LOVE SONGS OF VIDYĀPATI

I. MEETING OF EYES (15, 82)

LOVE SONGS
OF
VIDYĀPATI

———

TRANSLATED BY DEBEN BHATTACHARYA
EDITED WITH AN INTRODUCTION, NOTES AND COMMENTS
BY W. G. ARCHER

GROVE PRESS, INC., NEW YORK

TRANSLATOR'S NOTE

The greatness of Vidyāpati's songs depends on the fusion of natural phenomena such as lightning and clouds, the moon and the night lily, the lotus and the bee with the greatest of lovers, Rādhā and Krishna and their emotional reactions to love, anguish, passion, jealousy, joy and sorrow.

Love poems, in particular lyrics, do not translate well. Therefore, in trying to render Vidyāpati's songs into English, I have concentrated on the atmosphere of the originals rather than on scrupulously adhering to tiny detail. The poems, in their original versions, are often concerned with rhyme, internal echoes and play on meaning. None of these can be reproduced in word for word translation. In order to portray what I consider to be the spirit of the poems, I have sometimes had to condense Vidyāpati's lines, content myself with fragments or clarify what might otherwise seem too concise. Following the example of most commentators, I have, in general, omitted Vidyāpati's 'signature' lines. In the interest of meaning, I have added titles. It is hoped that with these qualifications, part, at least, of Vidyāpati's true poetic essence will reach the English reader.

DEBEN BHATTACHARYA

2. FEVER OF LOVE (9, 41)

3. 'HILLS OF GOLD' (2, 45)

4. 'HE IS MY WARMTH WHEN THE WINTER IS HARD' (13)

CONTENTS

ILLUSTRATIONS

'THE FACE OF MY LOVE' (14)

6. 'AS THE AUTUMN MOON' (21)

7.   KISSES (17   2, 60)

9.   'O FRIEND, WHY EVER DID I SEE HIM?' (82)

'KRISHNA PINES
FOR WANT OF YOU'
(23, 100)

10. 'MY LOVE IN A FOREIGN LAND' (28)

12. PETALS OF LOTUS (22, 31, 42, 44, 53, 6

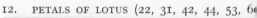

11. 'INSATIATE EYES' (15, 30)

INTRODUCTION

By W. G. ARCHER

The Indian poet, Vidyāpati, was born at Bisapi, a village in Madhubani, on the eastern side of north Bihar. 'Madhubani' means 'forest of honey' and the region with its great mango groves, fertile rice lands, fields of sugar-cane and lotus ponds provides a perfect environment for a poet. Its seasons range from winters of sparkling cold to springs and summers of exhilarating heat. In March and April, the cotton tree is afire with scarlet blossom. Evenings are bland and warm and at night people sleep outside their houses in the hot stillness. From late June to early September, vast clouds move across the sky. Days are either dark with rain, bright with steamy sunshine or livid with storm. By October the air is clear, the moon shines with dazzling brightness and at morning and evening the white peaks of the Himalayas stand along the skyline, enchanting in their frail etherial beauty. A hundred miles north of Bisapi stretch the low foot-hills of Nepal, covered with thick jungle and haunted by tiger. The country of Madhubani is part of Mithila, long renowned for its learning and culture. Its people are known as Maithils. It was in this part of India that Vidyāpati, a Maithil Brahmin, spent most of his life as courtier, scholar, writer and poet.

Although much discussed, the exact year of his birth is still uncertain, but opinion would now favour the year 1352.[1] At this time, Mithila was ruled by Hindu kings whose court adjoined present-day Darbhanga. Their independence was threatened by Muslim Sultanates and while escaping the indignity of Muslim occupation, they stood in restless subservience to the foreign power. Muslim armies occasionally appeared on the scene, battles occurred, tribute was exacted.

[1] For this and much other material concerning Vidyāpati, I am indebted to Subadra Jha, *The Songs of Vidyāpati* (Banaras, 1954).

17

Vidyāpati's father was attached to the court, though in what precise capacity we do not know. He seems to have been of a gentle retiring disposition, aloof from court intrigues and generally unconcerned either with his own career or that of his son. A devout Hindu, he is said to have besought Siva for the boon of a son and in response to have been granted Vidyāpati.

Vidyāpati's childhood and youth have not been recorded but as a Brahmin, a member of the priestly caste devoted to learning, he must early have been drilled in Sanskrit. He also mastered verse-making and perhaps through his father's influence hovered for a time on the fringes of the court. From Kirti Simha, the Maithil king who ruled from about 1370 to 1380, he received his first commission. This led to a long poem, the *Kirtilatā* or *Vine of Glory* in which he celebrated the royal house and magnified Kirti Simha's prowess. While praising the king, however, he could not totally refrain from hinting at his patron's deference to Muslims. His own early struggles are also suggested in some opening verses where he declares that poems are composed in every house, hearers exist in every village, critics in every town but patrons almost nowhere. The poem is mainly historical and a panegyric, but hints of the later love poet appear in a long passage glamorizing the courtesans of Delhi.

Kirti Simha extended no further patronage, but the *Vine of Glory* established Vidyāpati as a writer and under Kirti Simha's son, Deva Simha, he began residence at court. He was now accepted as a Sanskrit scholar and at Deva Simha's instance wrote a work of fiction, *Bhuparikramā* or *Around the World*. In this book, he imparted political and religious wisdom in the guise of romantic stories. Poetry, however, was becoming more and more important to him and his close friendship with the heir apparent, Siva Simha, was now to create the conditions in which he wrote more than five hundred love songs in Maithili.

These songs were new to Indian literature. They were songs as distinct from formal poems, but what is more, they broke with standard poetic convention. They were composed not in Sanskrit, but in Maithili. Sanskrit with its subtle inflections conveyed a sense of almost florid sophistication. Maithili was simple, musical and direct. It was the language spoken in the towns and villages of Mithila, but it had yet to be employed as a literary medium. Indeed it bore to Sanskrit the same relation as medieval Italian did to Latin. Vidyāpati frankly adopted it. He used it for poetry and by imbuing Sanskrit imagery with tender grace enchanted not only the learned, but the villagers. Such love songs had more than local significance. Behind them lay a whole tradition of Indian love-making and it was his roots in Sanskrit poetry which were to make Vidyāpati the greatest love poet of his time.

From the first century AD, Sanskrit love poetry had been marked by ardent sensuality and zest for Nature. As the lover contemplated his beloved, he was moved by certain qualities—her gentle tenderness, girlish passion, kind solicitude, eager devotion. He was stirred by the thought that she desired him and would brave all for his love. Indeed to be embraced by a loving girl was 'the height of all ambition'. At the same time he was sensitive to sexual charm and various objects drawn from Nature provided him with standards of beauty. Her eyes must be large and tender like a doe's. They should flash like lightning. Her face should dazzle like the moon and have the same serene pallor. Her skin, limbs and hands should be smooth and delicate like the leaf of a lotus. She herself should resemble a lotus flower in her delicate softness. Just as a lotus flower opens to the sun, a lovely girl should respond to her lover's gaze. Her breasts should be large and firm like pitchers of water or the fruits of *bel* trees. Her hair should be black as night and long as the tendrils of a vine. As a Sanskrit poet described a beauty, he would use again and again the same standard images as if any departure from the accepted list might imply some fault or blemish.

The same response to Nature determined how love itself should be described. Nature was regarded as the great kindler of desire—spring with its gathering heat providing an obvious analogy to the fever of passion. The moon streaming down was like a girl delighting in her love or a lover dazzling a girl. Bees avidly searching for blossom called to mind youthful gallants pursuing their loves. *Kokilas*, the cuckoos of Indian poetry, expressed with their shrill cries the brazen incitements of the season. Whatever was cool—moonlight, the wind, sandal-wood —was also sensuous and far from assuaging passion might also inflame it. Sun and moon, warmth and heat, clouds and wind

caressed the senses and as a result induced at times an almost
unbearable tumescence.

'The mango trees are a blaze of colour,
The new foliage flecked with coppery sheen
And their bursting blossoms,
Swinging as they list in the breeze,
Dazzle the minds of maids
And they catch their breath
With golden new excitement.

The clinging vine,
Whose lovely blossoms are kissed by the crazy
    bees
And whose soft tendrils aquiver
Bend in the gentle breeze,
Arrests the eyes of enamoured couples;
Sudden their hearts are filled
With the flowing stream of love.

In this flower-month
The hovering bee with the balmy spoil of honey,
The cuckoo with its melodious lilt
And the mango trees
With their glory of blossoms
Tempt the proud girl's mind
With stinging darts of the swoop of thought
Kindling the flame of love.

In the season of spring,
Ringing with the sweet birdsong of the cuckoo,
And the murmur of the wild bees,
Maidens, with their dangling girdles,
And roped gleam of necklace on the bosom,
Their supple limbs wholly relaxed
And subdued by the mighty strength of love
Enrapture by force
The hearts of men.'[1]

[1] Kālidāsa (fourth century AD), *The Seasons*. Trans. Pandit, 53, 62-5.

Even the forest was no mere trysting-place for lovers, but a sympathetic setting goading them to frenzy by its passionate analogies. As Rāma, hero of the first-century epic, the *Rāmā-yana*, wanders with his brother Lakshmana, searching for Sitā his beloved, the glamorous luxury of the forest scene provokes and taunts him.

'When Rāma went to the lake at Pampa he bewailed himself with mind awhirl. Scarce had he seen it but his senses quivered for joyful excitement; fallen under the power of the love-god he spoke these words: "Pampa is shining with its water clear as the cat's eye jewel, with its wealth of blooming day-lotuses and blue lotus-flowers, adorned with trees of many kinds. See the grove of Pampa, glorious to look at, how the trees rising as though to mountain heights, stand up like rocky steeps. But I, who am parched through with sorrow, I am tortured by agonies of soul. The flower-crowned creepers around us clasp everywhere the flower-laden trees. This season with its grateful wind, the scented moon of spring, when flowers and fruits have come forth on the trees, kindles a strong love.

' "Behold all the shapes of the rich-flowered forests, that shed a rain of flowers, as the clouds shed water. And on the lovely plains all the trees of the grove, shaken by the strength of the wind, bestrew the earth with blossoms. The wind issuing from the mountain-caves seems to sing, through the notes of the drunken *kokila*-bird, making the trees to dance. How grateful is its touch as it blows cool as sandal wood, bringing a pure scent and bearing weariness away. The trees sing with their wreaths of bees; their tops are roofed with flowers, buffeted by the tossing surge of the wind. With the song of the male *kokila*-bird, the trees resound, rousing to a fire the passion of my love. This fire—the spring whose embers are the flowery clusters of the *asoka* grove, whose crackling and roaring are the notes of the bees, whose red flames are the young shoots—this fire will burn me up. For life has no meaning for me if I do not see this woman with the soft-lashed eyes, the lovely hair and gentle speech.

' "I could bear the love that came to me, were it not that the spring, which brings the trees to blossom, wounds me so. I look at the lotus and its petals are the flower-cups of Sitā's eyes. Mingled with the threads of the lotus-flowers, the wind comes through the trees like Sitā's breath. The creepers follow the loved ones like drunken women, climbing from tree to tree, from rock to rock, from forest to forest. If my lovely one was here, if we could both dwell here, then should I not envy the king of the gods. For if I could joy with her on this soft and grassy floor I should be filled with care no more and long for nothing." [1]

So close a blending of love and Nature in one intermingling delight characterized Sanskrit love poetry for many centuries. But a second, more analytical approach was also current. In the third century, a treatise—the *Kāma Sutra* of Vātsyāyana— had treated love and sex from various angles. Men and women were classified into different physical types and varieties of sexual enjoyment were exhaustively discussed. At the same time lovers were analysed by role as well as by physique. Women in love were known as *nāyikās* and their lovers, *nāyakas*. Their complex attitudes towards each other and their varying moods and feelings were carefully differentiated. The result was a fund of knowledge which gave advice on how lovers should proceed, what conventions should be adopted, on the art, not so much of love-making, as of being in love.

(1)

'The rogue, seeing his twin loves on the same seat, came stealthily from behind and closing the eyes of one exhibited a lover's sporting trick. Then, turning his shoulder slightly, his hair bristling with joy, he kissed the other, her heart full of love and a suppressed smile playing on her cheeks.'

(2)

'Lying on the same bed with faces averted, suffering from each other's silence yet inwardly seeking submission, the couple wanted to preserve their prestige; but their eyes slowly met through covert glances and their love quarrel dissolved in laughter and embraces.'

(3)

'Moving to and fro her tender hands she gathers her garments. She throws towards the lamp what remains of the flower garland. Languid and smiling, she closes the eyes of her

[1] Vālmīki (first century AD), *Rāmāyana*. Quoted Meyer, II, 328–30.

husband. At the end of love-making, the charming girl again and again recalls their rapture.'[1]

Such Sanskrit love poetry was concerned with princes and their ladies, courtesans, 'men about town' and leisured gallants. It aimed at amusing a courtly class and took for granted a world of fashionable manners and daring encounters far removed from normal Indian practice. It was strictly secular. Indeed its nearest analogies in English are Shakespeare's sonnets and Elizabethan and Restoration love poetry. In the twelfth century, however, a change occurred—as if, in place of Shakespeare, the Biblical *Song of Songs* had suddenly become the leading model. This change was caused by the rising cult of Rādhā and Krishna and in order to understand its repercussions, first on Sanskrit love poetry and then on Vidyāpati, it is necessary to trace its development.

Until the early centuries AD, Krishna had been vaguely identified with the second member of the Hindu Trinity, Vishnu. In the sixth century, however, two books—the *Harivansa* (or *Genealogy of Krishna*) and the *Vishnu Purāna*—related his story and this was repeated in greater detail in a book of the ninth or tenth century, the *Bhāgavata Purāna*. According to this text, Vishnu as loving Preserver watched the struggle between gods and demons and the efforts of the wicked to discomfort the good. When the forces of evil appeared to triumph, he entered the world, slew demons and corrected the balance. He had intervened in this way on nine previous occasions and it was on the plea of Earth herself that he again took flesh and appeared as Krishna. His immediate goal was to slay a particular tyrant—a demon in human form—and thus encourage the good. For this purpose he was born into a princely family in the city of Mathura in northern India. Fearing the birth of his destroyer, the tyrant king had imprisoned Krishna's parents. To avoid the child's destruction they handed Krishna over to a family of wealthy cowherds. He was brought up in the forest of Brindaban, taught to graze cattle, play the flute and in general to live the life of a cowherd boy. During this time he warded off attacks from roving demons, aided the cowherds by the occasional exercise of supernatural powers and delighted

[1] Amaru (seventh century AD). Trans. Moti Chandra, 21, 23, 55.

both boys and girls and men and women by his strong magnetic charm. During this idyllic phase, he aroused love in the younger women and himself returned it. In ancient India girls were married early and Krishna's loves were therefore young married women with cowherd husbands. By employing his 'delusive power', Krishna kept their love secret, constantly met the cowgirls in the forest, and lavished his love upon them. Among the cowgirls Krishna had a special favourite but the *Bhāgavata Purāna* is at pains not to name her. Somewhat later, Krishna deemed his life among the cowherds to be over. He abandoned the cowgirls, returned to Mathura and slew the tyrant king. He was then readmitted to his family and, after inducing his clan to vacate Mathura, reinstalled them in a new city on the western seaboard at Dwarka. Here he married a number of queens, had children, killed further demons and lived the life of a feudal lord. Finally, holding his mission to be accomplished, he accepted death from a hunter's arrow and reunited himself with Vishnu.

These are salient details in a long and complicated story. It will be clear, however, that in the *Bhāgavata Purāna* Krishna appears in two distinct and even contradictory roles—as the lover of the cowgirls and as a feudal prince. The first role characterizes his youth, the second his manhood. Both are linked by the nature of his mission—to rid the world of demons —but the two Krishnas are obviously very different characters. The feudal prince supports established conventions and authority. The lover of the cowgirls puts love above everything. The prince demonstrates Vishnu's power; the cowherd, Vishnu's love. During the eleventh and twelfth centuries, this second Krishna became dominant, his role of lover was stressed, the name of his favourite, Rādhā, was frankly proclaimed and Krishna's love-making was interpreted as a symbol of the soul's union with God. To love Krishna, and by implication, Vishnu, was to achieve salvation and thus there arose a cult, the cult of Vaishnavism, in which the romance of Krishna with his favourite Rādhā was exalted as a means to spiritual release. In this version, it was conceded that Krishna from time to time went away, but his life as feudal prince was ignored and his whole career was made to focus on Rādhā. His loves, the other cowgirls, were not denied, but they were used to throw into greater relief his basic romance. In portraying all his loves as married women, the story emphasized the supremacy of love over duty and the need of the soul to allow nothing—not even morals—to stand between itself and God. Salvation was to be attained through love and praise of Krishna, the chanting of songs recounting his deeds and the constant celebration of his love for Rādhā. Amongst the strongholds of this new cult was Bengal, just east of Vidyāpati's home and it was there, towards the end of the twelfth century, that the poet Jayadeva made his great contribution to Sanskrit love poetry, the *Gita Govinda* or Song of Krishna.

In this poem, Jayadeva takes the Sanskrit tradition of courtly love poetry and applies it to Rādhā and Krishna. There is the same refined sensuality with its response to female charm. Love, nature and the seasons are intricately blended. There is the old analysis of mood and situation. What is different is the investment of the chief actors with other-worldly status. Rādhā and Krishna behave as ordinary lovers. They exploit to the full the Indian art of love. They delight in each other's beauty and experience a whole range of ardent emotions. But they are now distinct characters—they possess names—and behind their practices is the sanction of a great religious revival. Krishna is a *nāyaka*, a lover, but because he is also God or Vishnu, sexual love and passion are regarded as life at its most sublime. Praise of love-making becomes praise of Krishna. Praise of Krishna involves praise of love-making.

'Her face, a moon, is fondled by the fluttering petals in her hair,
The exciting moisture of his lips induces languor in her limbs—
Very large her passion blossoms with the closing of her eyes—
Beautiful her body with the drops of sweat through love's
    exertion,
She who is unswerving in love's conflict, fallen on his breast—
A certain girl, excelling in her charms unrivalled, dallies with
    the sportive Krishna.

In the blowing of a gentle breeze Krishna departs for the tryst;
What greater pleasure than this, my friend, to be found in the
    world anywhere?

Your beautiful breast with its shape like a jar, why should it
serve no end,
Your breast so full of passion and firmer than fruits of the
palmyra palm?
That exceedingly charming one, avoid him not, that beautiful
Krishna!
Through every stage of your love, and now, how much have I
spoken of this!
Cause your eyes to do their work by seeing Krishna beside you,
Krishna, lying in your bed, all cool, of lotus petals moist.

O you with your gentle voice, but speak! With lac I shall redden
the soles of your feet and make them glisten with oil,
Your pair of feet surpassing hibiscus flowers, delighting my
heart, your feet unrivalled in amorous play.
As an ornament place upon my head your feet, as a cure for the
venom of desire!
O let your feet remove the change now made by the pitiless fire
of love, which burns and which destroys!
With your languorous eyes, your glistening mouth like the
moon, your gait the thief of the heart, your thighs excelling
the trunk of the plantain;
With your skilful amorous play, with the sweet and beautiful
streaks of your eye-brows;
How wonderful, slender one, though on earth, the way you
bear in your person the nymphs of heaven!

She looked on Krishna who desired only her, on him who for
long wanted dalliance,
Whose face with his pleasure was overwhelmed and who was
possessed with desire
Who engendered passion with his face made lovely through
tremblings of glancing eyes
Like a pond in autumn with a pair of wagtails at play in a full-
blown lotus
Whose body was thrilling all over, restless, because of his skill
in love.'[1]

[1] Keyt, 63-4, 77, 82-4, 91-3.

26

Such passages were regarded by Jayadeva from two points of view. They were expressions in poetry of delight in love; but they were also 'praises of Krishna', praises which through sheer poetic intensity and verbal power could win their author and his audience eternal merit. Their potency, he insisted, derived not merely from what was praised, but from the verbal quality of the praise itself. Without his own poetic mastery, the subject, Krishna, would be insufficient. Yet without that subject, the poetry could not have existed. And in a series of lines inserted in the poem Jayadeva makes plain his overriding purpose.

'The seat of whose heart is adorned by the grace of Speech
Jayadeva the poet this poem created
Composed of the stories of Krishna's amorous play.
If in recalling Krishna to mind there is flavour
And if there is interest in love's art,
Then to this necklace of words—sweetness, brightness,
        tenderness—
The words of Jayadeva, listen!'

(*Prelude*)

'This glowing song, auspicious blessing, causing pleasure and
        gladness,
Was made by the poet Shri Jayadeva.'

(*Prelude*)

'This, the description—the forest in spring-time, delightful—
        threaded with phases of passion,
The purpose of which is to recollect Krishna, wells up in
        utterance of Shri Jayadeva.'

(*Canto* 1)

'O make him enjoy me, my friend, that Krishna so fickle,
And may he playfully make more pleasure, sung here by Shri
        Jayadeva
Describing his many and endless amours with amorous herd
        women.'

(*Canto* 2)

'May it bring more bliss, this Shri Jayadeva's
Song that has reached the foot of Krishna!'

(*Canto* 4)

'Give his place in your heart to Krishna, when the poet
    Jayadeva has spoken.'

(*Canto* 5)

'O worship Krishna, to be welcomed in resembling merit, and
    who shows so much mercy to
'His devotee, the poet Shri Jayadeva, who now makes this
    utterance of a very lovely song!'

(*Canto* 5)

'Where people delight in song may joy
Be spread with this poem of Shri Jayadeva!'

(*Canto* 6)

'May the sport of Krishna's amours in the song of Shri
    Jayadeva
Bring completely to an end the sins of this age.'

(*Canto* 7)

'May this song of Jayadeva dwell upon the necks of people
Given to Krishna, necks the beauty of their necklaces
    surpassing.'

(*Canto* 11)

'O people, place Krishna for ever in your hearts, Krishna the
    source of all merit,
By whom, in the wealth of Jayadeva's poem, all beauty of art
    has been doubled!'

(*Canto* 11)

'Among all tasteful people may this song of Jayadeva create
    a state of passionate delight,
The poem which in every verse proclaims the satisfaction in
    the pleasure of the love of Krishna.'

(*Canto* 12)

'Whatever is of the condition of love's discernment shown
with beauty in poetic form, and all skill in the art of
heaven's musicians, and all of reflection on Vishnu,
All such you may joyfully see, wise people, in this the song of
the Lord of Herds, made by the poet devoted to
him, the wise Jayadeva.'

(Canto 12)[1]

Throughout the poem, Jayadeva's devotion to Krishna, delight
in love, awareness of Nature and belief in poetry are equally
strong. And although Vidyāpati's achievement is somewhat
different, it was the influence on his work of some of these
qualities which was to earn for him the title, 'the new Jayadeva'.

The love songs of Vidyāpati were composed almost two hundred
years after Jayadeva and like the earlier writer's poem were
ostensibly concerned with Rādhā and Krishna. Each song deals
with an aspect of their relationship, a situation or a moment of
crisis. In certain verses Vidyāpati addresses Rādhā or Krishna
direct. In others he sees them through the eyes of a confidant
or friend. At times he acts as an observer, patiently describing
Rādhā's symptoms when parted from her lover, or vividly
evoking her ecstasy as she lies in Krishna's arms. Often the
lovers are not expressly named, but even when seemingly
anonymous they are none the less Rādhā and Krishna. We can
readily understand how in terms of subject Vidyāpati may have
seemed an incarnation of his great precursor.

Yet despite this similarity, his love songs differ in two important respects. The *Gita Govinda* is, in essence, a poetic
drama. It begins with a crisis in Rādhā and Krishna's
romance. It shows Krishna abandoning Rādhā for the
cowgirls, experiencing remorse and then begging forgiveness.
Rādhā repulses him, but in turn is overcome with guilt
and the drama ends with their rapturous reunion. In its
twelve cantos, each with a separate melody, different emotions
and situations are interpreted, but each takes its place in a
single logical scheme. In Vidyāpati's work, each song is separate
and detached. It is meant to be sung alone. It illuminates the
great romance, but avoids all sense of gathering drama. Like the

[1] Keyt.

various parts of T. S. Eliot's *The Waste Land*, the songs are consistent in theme, but are otherwise unconnected.

Their second difference is in attitude. In adoring God as Krishna, Jayadeva inevitably sees the romance through Krishna's eyes. Despite the cantos devoted to Rādhā's anguish, it is Krishna's prowess as a lover which is constantly praised. Jayadeva is strongly susceptible to womanly charm, but he regards it from Krishna's attitude, that of the male lover. Rādhā's function is to love Krishna, to be 'enjoyed' by him, and from this point of view, Jayadeva accords her the lower or lesser role. Although she is portrayed suffering all the ache of separation, this is more as a tribute to Krishna's magnetism than out of real sympathy for her. He has only to apologize and, if the apology is not immediately accepted, Rādhā is promptly accused of sulking and of being needlessly 'proud'. 'Give up this baseless pride against me' Krishna is made to say, and it is clear that Jayadeva feels that a woman should regard herself as supremely fortunate to receive male caresses at all. To Krishna, the ideal lover, on the other hand, love-making is a due, a right, an activity to be pursued with ruthless vigour. It is Krishna's amorous play, therefore, not Rādhā's, which is celebrated by Jayadeva and although their love-making is throughout described with fervour, it is always for Krishna that the fullest appreciation is reserved. 'May pure and unclouded joy and prosperity come from this movement of hands of the Best of Men, amorous hands delighting in breasts, hands in performance of many forms of amorous play with Rādhā beside the Jamnā.' Krishna's hands, not Rādhā's breasts, are the true subject of Jayadeva's poetry.

In contrast to this robustly male approach, Vidyāpati is almost feminine. It is true that in his songs Krishna is the lover, but the quality of ecstatic praise, of intense and personal devotion is wanting. Krishna is accepted for what he is—a delightful charmer, a marvellous lover. But he is not presented as a hero nor as a person to whom the poet himself offers adoring admiration. He is even regarded as callous, cruel, selfish, the very opposite of one who naturally inspires devotion, sympathy and appreciation. Rādhā, on the other hand, is Vidyāpati's true heroine. Her career as a young girl, her slowly awakening youth, her physical charm, her shyness, doubts and hesitations, her naïve innocence, her need for love, her surrender to rapture, her utter anguish when neglected—all these are described from the woman's point of view and with matchless tenderness. Vidyāpati, it is evident, loved and admired the female temperament and nature. Its softness and delicacy stirred his deepest feelings and he could not bear to see girls and women affronted in love or their loving dispositions cruelly wounded. He assumed that sexual love was the greatest need and experience in life. But it was meant as much for women as for men. Women were made for love but they were gentle and sensitive and only by respecting their soft refinement could they be truly loved. At the same time, Vidyāpati understood men and while the male mind did not interest him as keenly as did the female, he did not blind himself to masculine traits—the need for sex, the male interest in women, the violent nature of male desire. These, it seemed to him, were facts and girls and women must somehow come to terms with them. Even, therefore, when he is stressing Rādhā's soft and delicate nature, he sometimes pulls himself up with a jerk, as if he feels that too much sympathy and understanding are not in a woman's own interests and that even a sensitive girl must be tough with herself. He oscillates, in fact, between a quite exceptional appreciation of feminine delicacy and a robust 'stand no nonsense' attitude. For the girl who was unused to sex he displayed the greatest understanding and some of his most remarkable verses stress the chagrin which Rādhā feels when lack of experience causes her to leave her lover disappointed. For experienced girls, on the other hand, he took the view that it was impossible for them to be over-loved and that any protests to the contrary were sheer humbug. Vidyāpati evidently understood his own bias for he sometimes inserted in the final couplet of a song a dry man-of-the-worldish comment intended to serve as a corrective. He concluded, for example, a description by Rādhā of her rapture, with the words, 'Says Vidyāpati: How can I possibly believe such nonsense?' But it was because Vidyāpati did in fact believe this 'nonsense' that his songs had their wide appeal.

Vidyāpati's love songs seem to have been composed between about the year 1380 and 1406. But the poet did not die until 1448 and until a few years prior to his death he was still writing.

His main works were complicated treatises in Sanskrit and although he did not totally abandon song-writing in Maithili, his Maithili poetry after 1406 comprised hymns to Siva, Vishnu, Durgā and Gangā. Songs about Rādhā and Krishna were abruptly abandoned and the love poet became once more the distinguished Sanskritist, learned scholar and director of studies. So sudden a cessation demands an explanation and in examining the circumstances which may have prompted his love poetry we may also gain a further clue to its meaning and significance.

We have seen that a vital factor in Vidyāpati's development was his association and friendship with Siva Simha, king of Mithila from 1402 to 1406, and for some time previous its actual ruler. The depth of this friendship is attested by several facts. In 1402, shortly after his formal accession to the Maithil throne, Siva Simha presented Vidyāpati with his native village of Bisapi, the copper-plate which recorded the grant referring to him as 'the new Jayadeva'. This grant is clear proof of royal esteem and can only have been made on the basis of lively appreciation. In many of his songs, Vidyāpati introduces into the concluding line a reference to his patron. The only patron included in these love songs, however, is Siva Simha and this fact is itself sufficient to show how special was their relationship. But it is a third circumstance which proves how close were the two men. The Muslim Emperor is supposed to have summoned Siva Simha to Delhi to answer a charge. Vidyāpati went with him. When Siva Simha was arraigned before the Emperor, Vidyāpati bargained for his release by offering to display his clairvoyance. The Emperor locked the poet in a wooden box and sent a posse of courtesans to bathe in the river. When the bathing was over, Vidyāpati was released and asked to describe what had happened. He immediately recited one of his verses describing a beautiful woman at her bath. The Emperor was so stunned at the coincidence that he pardoned Siva Simha and the two returned to Mithila.

Yet if Siva Simha's active interest in Vidyāpati provided the poet with favouring conditions, we have still to understand why he wrote love songs in Maithili and cast Rādhā and Krishna as ideal lovers. To this, a first answer can be found in the contemporary situation in neighbouring Bengal. Until the thirteenth century, every Hindu court had gloried in keeping Sanskrit scholars—'gifted men whose contempt for Bengali was as great as was their scholarship in Sanskrit'. With the coming of the Pathans, however, all this had changed. 'The Pathans occupied Bengal early in the thirteenth century. They came from a far distance—from Balkh, Oxus or Transoxina, but they settled in the plains of Bengal and had no mind to return to their mountainous home. The Pathan Emperors learned Bengali and lived in close touch with the teeming Hindu population whom they were called upon to rule. The minarets and cupolas of their mosques rose to the sky, adjoining the spires and tridents of the Hindu temples. The sounds of the conch-shells and bells emanating from the latter were heard while the newcomers assembled in the mosques to say their evening prayers. The Emperors heard of the far-reaching fame of the Sanskrit epics, the Rāmāyana and the Mahābhārata, and observed the wonderful influence which they exercised in moulding the religious and domestic life of the Hindus, and they naturally felt a desire to be acquainted with the contents of these poems. The Pathan Emperors and Chiefs could not have the great patience of the Hindu kings who were inspired by a religious zeal to hear the Brahmin scholars recite Sanskrit texts and their learned annotations, step by step, requiring the listeners many long years to complete a course of lectures on the Rāmāyana or the Mahābhārata. They appointed scholars to translate the works into Bengali which they now spoke and understood. The first Bengali translation of the Mahābhārata of which we hear was undertaken at the order of Nasirā Sāhā, the Emperor of Gaur, who ruled for forty years till 1325 AD.

'Instances of like nature, where Muhammadan Emperors and Chiefs initiated and patronized translations of Sanskrit and Persian works into Bengali, are numerous, and we are led to believe, that when the powerful Moslem Sovereigns of Bengal granted this recognition to the vernacular language in their courts, Hindu Rajas naturally followed suit. The Brahmins could not resist the influence of this high patronage; they were therefore compelled to favour the language they had hated so much, and latterly they themselves came forward to write poems and compile works of translation in Bengali.'[1]

[1] Sen, 10–14.

Fashion alone, however, can hardly explain Vidyāpati's love-songs and it is rather the place of ladies in Siva Simha's court and palace which seems to have been the deciding factor. Like other princes of the time, Siva Simha had several consorts and also regaled himself with dancing girls. He was alive to sensual excitement, yet possessed a very real admiration for his various queens. The senior queen was Lakhimā Devi and it was perhaps to entertain and delight the ladies of Siva Simha as well as the prince himself that Vidyāpati not only wrote love songs but wrote them in Maithili, a language which they could immediately understand. If we assume a courtly atmosphere in which love was greatly valued and ladies also played a prominent part, we may well approach the conditions in which Vidyāpati composed. It is certainly remarkable that in many of his concluding couplets (the *bhanitās*, as they were termed) Vidyāpati addresses his patron not simply as Siva Simha but as Siva Simha, husband of one or other of his queens.

'Says Vidyāpati: Be bold and you will have your way. Raja Siva Simha knows this mood. He embodies every sentiment in the company of Soram Devi.'

'Says Vidyāpati: Only a great lover can attract this lovely woman. Raja Siva Simha, husband of Hāsini Devi, is blessed by Krishna.'

'Says Vidyāpati: Raja Siva Simha knows very well this mood. He is the fine husband of Madhumati Devi.'

In these lines, three queens—Soram Devi, Hāsini Devi and Madhumati Devi—are each mentioned and Siva Simha is praised as being their husband.

But it was the senior queen, Lakhimā Devi, who was most frequently invoked by Vidyāpati.

'Says the poet Vidyāpati: Young girl, be brave, Raja Siva Simha is the fine husband of Lakhimā Devi.'

'Says Vidyāpati, skilled in all moods: Love has no limits. Raja Siva Simha is the husband of Lakhimā Devi.'

'Raja Siva Simha, god-like in form, is the husband of Lakhimā.'

'Says the poet Vidyāpati: In this universe of three worlds, there is none like him. Raja Siva Simha, god-like in form, is the husband of Lakhimā Devi.'

So determined a linking of Siva Simha's name with that of a queen, especially with that of Lakhimā Devi, suggests a court atmosphere in which ladies could thrive and where the personality of each was much appreciated. Siva Simha must certainly have relished his ladies as characters and persons and in these very revealing lines Vidyāpati sets them almost on a parity with the prince himself.

It is possibly this unusual court atmosphere which led Vidyāpati to cast Rādhā and Krishna as prime lovers in the songs. There is no evidence that he himself was a special devotee of Krishna. Unlike Jayadeva, he did not worship Krishna as the prime means to salvation. There is also no evidence that he was a Vaishnava in the sense of being a practising member of the Vaishnava cult. Indeed all his later writings ignore Rādhā and Krishna and it is rather on Siva and Durgā that he lavishes attention. Even when he concerns himself with Vishnu, it is Vishnu himself, not Krishna, who is invoked. He seems, in fact, to have been an orthodox Maithil for even in present-day Mithila it is this attitude which still prevails. Krishna is honoured as one of the gods and on the occasion of his birthday, an archway is erected in each village to enshrine his effigy. But there is no chanting of hymns of praise, no mention of Rādhā and no singing of Rādhā–Krishna songs. Krishna takes his place in the Hindu pantheon not as the supreme means of salvation but as a lesser figure dwarfed by Siva, Vishnu and Durgā. Only, in fact, at weddings are songs of Rādhā and Krishna sung and then less for their spiritual significance than as guides to married love. It is as ideal lovers rather than as God that their names are invoked.

This attitude was possibly suggested to Vidyāpati by a Sanskrit work, the *Gāthāsaptasati* in which the same treatment was adopted, Rādhā and Krishna assuming the roles of the *nāyikās* and *nāyakas* of Sanskrit tradition and for the rest being indistinguishable from their secular counterparts. But it was the fancied resemblance of Siva Simha's court to Krishna's life in Brindaban which may have prompted Vidyāpati to place his love songs in a Rādhā–Krishna setting. If Siva Simha is treated as another Krishna—handsome, charming, delighting in ladies—Lakhimā Devi would correspond to Rādhā, his chief love, while his other queens and court ladies would represent the various cowgirls with whom Krishna also made love. If Siva Simha's interest in love is conceded and if he was also a great lover, then this identification with Krishna would be a subtle form of courtly flattery. That a connection with Krishna is implied seems clear from a *bhanitā* in one of Vidyāpati's songs. The song concerns a girl unable to contain her longing and the poet remarks, 'Says Vidyāpati: O young girl, full of every quality, the date expires today. The husband of Lakhimā Devi will fulfil your desire. Raja Siva Simha will come.' It is true that these words refer to the poet's patron, but it is to Krishna, 'fulfiller of desire', that they would more normally have been addressed. In casting Siva Simha for this role, Vidyāpati is, in fact, treating him as Krishna.

During all these years of creative activity, Siva Simha played a vital part in Vidyāpati's song-writing. So entranced was he by the songs that he attached a special singer, Jayata, to the poet, and, as song after song was composed, Jayata would decide which tune should be employed. He would then sing the songs before Siva Simha and his ladies. The vernacular words and their tunes would stick in their minds. Dancing-girls learnt them, and from being a court product they spread across all Mithila. The songs, however, concerned a set of persons. They were related to a special court and assumed a special situation. So long as Siva Simha ruled, Vidyāpati composed. But in 1406 a disaster befell and with this cataclysm his lyric impulses faded. In this year Muslim armies appeared. Siva Simha and his forces gave battle. They were routed and Siva Simha vanished. Since his body was not recovered, it was thought at first that he must have fled. Yet news of his flight was lacking and his end remained a mystery. For the time being, Lakhimā Devi, members of the household and Vidyāpati himself sought refuge with a Raja in Nepal. Some time later Lakhimā Devi returned to Mithila and for twelve years acted as Regent. When, after this long period, there was still no news, her devotion to Siva Simha was so intense that it led her to adopt the customary course.

Giving him up as dead, she made a grass effigy of her husband and burnt herself on a funeral pyre.

For Vidyāpati the years succeeding Siva Simha's disappearance were filled with tragic gloom. His patron's fate took the heart out of his writing. If in seemingly writing of Rādhā and Krishna, he was, in fact, writing of Siva Simha and his court, the vital condition snapped. At Rajabanauli in Nepal he lived in lonely isolation, completing in 1408 for the local Raja a Sanskrit work, the *Likhanāvali* (*How to write letters in Sanskrit*). Ten years later, he made a complete copy in his own hand of a manuscript of the *Bhāgavata Purāna*. In 1418, Padma Simha succeeded Lakhimā Devi as ruler of Mithila and about this time Vidyāpati seems once again to have joined the court. His pre-eminence as a Sanskrit scholar was fully recognized and although over sixty he produced one learned treatise after another. In one, *The Essence of Siva*, he described Siva worship. Another was called *Garlands of Words for Gangā*. Others discuss the law of inheritance and division of property, fasts and festivals observed during the year and offerings made to dead relations at Gaya. Yet a sixth, written at the instance of Raja Nara Simha, was entitled *The River of Devotion to Durgā*. All these works are tributes to his learning, but only in his hymns to Siva, Vishnu, Durgā and Gangā does the poet appear. How far these later songs compare with the earlier as poetry it is difficult to decide, but it would be tempting to see Vidyāpati as an Indian Donne, expressing in his late religious verse the same ardent rapture which earlier had found expression in the poetry of love.

In about 1430 or a little later, Vidyāpati retired from court life and returned to Bisapi, his village. There he often visited the temple to Siva. He was now extremely old, yet his years of glory, spent with Siva Simha, were ever in his mind. In 1438 his patron appeared to him in a dream and Vidyāpati viewed it as a portent of his approaching death. He is believed to have died ten years later, aged ninety-six.

Although it is unlikely that Vidyāpati composed love songs after the disaster of 1406, it is as a love poet that he has ever since been honoured in Mithila. Indeed as he advanced in years, he must have found the situation somewhat ironical—his songs sung everywhere, people enchanted by their Maithili sweetness, while he himself had drily reverted to learning and scholarship. Even today Vidyāpati's love songs are treasured by Maithil ladies and are constantly sung at weddings. When a new bride goes to her husband's house, one of the first questions which other ladies ask her is 'What songs by Vidyāpati do you know?' As celebrations of love from a woman's point of view, they have enchanted countless households in Mithila and are likely to do so as long as its ancient culture lasts.

In Bengal, Vidyāpati's use of Rādhā and Krishna as ideal lovers led many Bengalis to regard him as a Vaishnava. Bengali scholars visiting Mithila brought back copies of his songs. Chaitanya (1456–1534), the first propounder of modern Vaishnavism in eastern India—the form in which Rādhā–Krishna is regarded as the highest deity—freely adopted the songs as Vaishnava hymns. Chandidās, another writer of Rādhā and Krishna songs, also viewed Vidyāpati as a supreme contributor to the same devotional tradition. In one extreme sect, the fact that he had included Lakhimā Devi in certain songs led to the inference that he had been secretly in love with her and had carried on an intrigue. He thereby qualified to rank as one of the sect's seven *rasikabhaktas* (or 'devotees of love'). Others believed that Vidyāpati was a Bengali, not a Maithil, and that he could only compose songs when Lakhimā was present. 'Lakhimā is Rādhā, the supreme goddess; as soon as she is seen, poetry springs forth in a hundred streams.' There is no apparent basis for any of these legends, yet their very existence testifies to Vidyāpati's greatness as a poet and the appeal of Rādhā and Krishna to Hindu India.

In the West, Vidyāpati's poetry is still unknown—a few translations by Coomaraswamy, Arun Sen and Sir George Grierson being all that have so far appeared. Yet, perhaps more than at any other time, his poems can now be appreciated. In the twentieth century, western understanding of sexual love has been extended by the poems of T. S. Eliot and the novels of Ernest Hemingway, D. H. Lawrence, Graham Greene and Lawrence Durrell. To those aware of modern literature, it may come as something of a shock that living long before Shakespeare, in the Middle Ages, an Indian poet also should have shown so deep an understanding of modern love.

W. G. ARCHER

SIGNS OF YOUTH

Rādhā's glances dart from side to side.
Her restless body and clothes are heavy with dust.
Her glistening smile shines again and again.
Shy, she raises her skirt to her lips.
Startled, she stirs and once again is calm,
As now she enters the ways of love.
Sometimes she gazes at her blossoming breasts
Hiding them quickly, then forgetting they are there.
Childhood and girlhood melt in one
And new and old are both forgotten.

Says Vidyāpati: O Lord of life,
Do you not know the signs of youth?

'Heavy with dust.' Rādhā has felt so restless that she has not cared where she went or sat. Because of this her body and clothes have become dirty with dust.

TANGLED TRESSES

Each day the breasts of Rādhā swelled.
Her hips grew shapely, her waist more slender.
Love's secrets stole upon her eyes.
Startled, her childhood sought escape.
Her plum-like breasts grew large,
Harder and crisper, aching for love.
Krishna soon saw her as she bathed,
Her filmy dress still clinging to her breasts,
Her tangled tresses falling on her heart,
A golden image swathed in yak's tail plumes.

Says Vidyāpati: O wonder of women,
Only a handsome man can long for her.

'Yak's tail plumes' are Rādhā's hair, the 'golden image' her glowing skin.

On yaks, Pandit comments, '*Chamara* is the bushy tail of the Tibetan animal, the yak, *Bos grunniens*, which is itself known as *chamari*. The tail is used as a fly-whisk. The yak is a splendid beast with short legs, low quarters, warmly clad in long hair, and furnished with a bushy tail which serves him as a wind-screen, the herd always feeding with its hind-quarters to the wind. The yak will carry anything that a horse can, climb almost everywhere that a goat can and can cross a river with the ease of a hippopotamus. He is to the high altitude nomad what the camel is to the Arab of the low-lying desert. The huge white tail of the yak together with the white parasol have formed the insignia of royalty from ancient times. The Hindi *chauri*, for a fly-whisk, is derived from *chamara*.'

The tail with its long silky hairs was used for gently stirring the air or lightly dusting an idol or image.

FIRST RAPTURE

There was a shudder in her whispering voice.
She was shy to frame her words.
What has happened tonight to lovely Rādhā?
Now she consents, now she is afraid.
When asked for love, she closes up her eyes,
Eager to reach the ocean of desire.
He begs her for a kiss.
She turns her mouth away
And then, like a night lily, the moon seized her.
She felt his touch startling her girdle.
She knew her love treasure was being robbed.
With her dress she covered up her breasts.
The treasure was left uncovered.

Vidyāpati wonders at the neglected bed.
Lovers are busy in each other's arms.

'The moon seized her.' On account of its dazzling beauty, the moon is an obvious symbol for Krishna or the lover.

Pandit points out that in Sanskrit poetry, as in German, the moon is masculine.

> The moon, long gazing, at will,
> At the faces of lovely women
> Sweetly slumbering on whitened terraces
> At night, is doubtless over-eager.
> (KĀLIDĀSA, *The Seasons*)

In Indian thought and usage, the breasts were regarded as the prime seat of modesty. Rādhā's instinctive reaction, therefore, is to keep them covered, despite other more fateful consequences.

4

DAWN

Awake, Rādhā, awake,
Calls the parrot and its love.
For how long must you sleep,
Clasped to the heart of your Dark-stone?
Listen. The dawn has come
And the red shafts of the sun
Are making us shudder. . . .

Parrots were often kept in cages from where they could witness lovers' intimate encounters. Their role as confidant, protector, witness and friend is illustrated in two poems by Amaru, the Sanskrit poet of the seventh century.

'Whatever words were uttered by the couple during the night were overheard by the parrot who loudly repeated them to the elders. Hearing such an overflow of words, the flurried lady took a ruby ear-ring, like the seed of a pomegranate, and dangled it before its beak.

' "Give me food, otherwise I will loudly proclaim your whole secret." When the house parrot slowly said this, the lady bashfully turned her face away, laughed to herself and looked like a half-blown lotus bent by the wind.' (Trans. Moti Chandra)

In the poem, the parrot's intervention is due to the familiar dawn situation. Lovers who have spent the night in each other's arms, shielded by darkness, must abruptly separate to avoid detection.

'Dark-stone' was a mythical jewel and hence, on account of Krishna's blue colour, an apt analogy for the god.

THE NECKLACE SNAKE

Listen, O lovely darling,
Cease your anger.
I promise by the golden pitchers of your breasts
And by your necklace-snake,
Which now I gather in my hands,
If ever I touch anyone but you
May your necklace bite me;
And if my words do not ring true,
Punish me as I deserve.
Bind me in your arms, bruise me with your thighs,
Choke my heart with your milk-swollen breasts,
Lock me day and night in the prison of your heart.

Pitchers were constantly used in Indian poetry as symbols for the
breasts.

RIVER AND SKY

O friend, I cannot tell you
Whether he was near or far, real or a dream.
Like a vine of lightning,
As I chained the dark one,
I felt a river flooding in my heart.
Like a shining moon,
I devoured that liquid face.
I felt stars shooting around me.
The sky fell with my dress,
Leaving my ravished breasts.
I was rocking like the earth.
In my storming breath
I could hear my ankle-bells,
Sounding like bees.
Drowned in the last waters of dissolution,
I knew that this was not the end.

Says Vidyāpati:
How can I possibly believe such nonsense?

The dark one' is Krishna.

'The last waters of dissolution' refers to the deluge which in Hindu thought is supposed to end each world cycle. When one cycle has ended, another commences.

For the phrase 'I was rocking like the earth', compare Ernest Hemingway, *For Whom the Bell Tolls*, where a lover asks 'Did the earth move?' and the girl replies 'Yes. It moved.'

FEAR AND LOVE

O friend, friend, take me with you.
I am only a young girl,
No one can stop him
So violent a lover is he.
My heart shudders to go near him.
How the black-bee ravishes the lotus-bud.
For hours,
He crushes my frail body
Quivering like a drop of water
On a lotus leaf.
How long must I endure the curse of life?
Which god invented that she-demon night?

Vidyāpati says: Who can believe you?
Do you not see that dawn is coming?

Night is a 'she-demon' because it is the source of so much ecstasy
and so much torment.

'Who can believe you?' The assumption is that no girl or woman
can be too much loved. To pretend otherwise is rubbish.

For a long account of the bee as symbol of the lover, see Verrier
Elwin and Shamrao Hivale, *Folk-Songs of the Maikal Hills*.

TORMENT

O friend, how can I say what happened in the night?
Mādhava was torture.
Thrusting his fingers on my breasts
He drank my lips.
Pressing his face hard on mine,
He took my life away.
His youthful strength
So wantonly aroused
Drugged his senses.
A country boy,
He did not know
The art of love.
I prayed and begged in vain.

Vidyāpati says:
My dear lady,
You are enchanted by that greedy god.

'Mādhava', 'the honied one', is a synonym for Krishna.

'A country boy' or rustic would naturally be rough and crude.
Having been reared among the cowherds of Brindaban, Krishna is
exposed to such a taunt.

As in other poems, Vidyāpati is not disposed to treat Rādhā's
grievance seriously—violence being a necessary part of passionate
love and no woman, in his view, ever truly disliking it.

BROODING LOVE

Mādhava:
Your moon-faced love
Had never guessed
That parting hurts.
Rādhā is tortured,
Dreading you will leave.
Love has robbed her of all power,
She sinks clasping the ground.

Kokilas call,
Startled, she wakes
Only to brood again.
Tears wash the make-up
From her breasts.
Her arms grow thin,
Her bracelets slide to the ground.
Rādhā's head droops in grief.
Her fingers scar the earth
Bleeding your name.

Like the English cuckoo, the *kokila* or *koel* (*Eudynamis scolopaceus*) is the typical 'bird of spring', its appearance heralding the hot weather—the spring of India. It is also a parasite on other birds, in this case the Common House Crow.

In English poetry, this practice by the cuckoo accounts for the word 'cuckoldry', the phrase 'the slanderous cuckoo' and for Shakespeare's song

> The cuckoo then, on every tree,
> Mocks married men, for thus sings he,
> 'Cuckoo, cuckoo!'
> O word of fear,
> Unpleasing to the married ear.

—unpleasing since it implies, for the husband, an invasion of his home, the rearing of children not his own and hence, adultery.

In India, this aspect of the *kokila* or *koel* seems to have passed unnoticed and the bird is rather admired for its handsome sheen and soaring cry.

Since the spring or hot weather is connected with love, the cries of *kokilas* incite desire and are therefore intolerable to lonely women parted from their lovers.

TOMORROW

He left me saying he would be back tomorrow.
I've covered the floor of my home
Writing: Tomorrow.
When dawn came, they all enquired:
Tell us, friend,
When will your tomorrow come?
Tomorrow, tomorrow, I gave up my hopes,
My beloved never returned.

Says Vidyāpati, listen, beautiful one,
Other women held him back.

As in other poems, Vidyāpati's comment is partly intended as a
mocking jest, partly as a reminder of her previous good fortune in
having had a lover who is in such great demand.

SHATTERED DESIRE

Swelling breasts, hard, like golden cups.
Those wanton glances have stolen my heart,
O beautiful one, protest no longer.
I am eager as a bee, let me take your honey.
Darling, I beg you, holding your hands,
Do not be cruel, have pity on me.
I shall say that again and again,
No more can I suffer the agony of love.

Says Vidyāpati:
Shattered desire is death.

From very early times it was recognized in India that unappeased love might lead to death. The standard treatise on the art and science of love, *The Kāma Sutra* (third century AD), expressly conceded that adultery and extra-marital love might sometimes be necessary in order to save life.

FROWNS AND SMILES

When my lover comes to my courtyard,
I shall smile and move away.
Frantic, he will catch my dress,
Yet I shall not relent.
When he begs me for love,
I shall smile but not speak.
As he darts at my bodice,
I shall stop him with my hands and scolding eyes.
Distraught, the beautiful bee will seize my chin,
Suck honey from my lips,
And loot my senses.

By convention, a lonely woman is supposed to feign resentment or displeasure at the lover's advances.

RETURNING LOVER

O friend, there is no end to my joy!
Mādhava is home for ever.
The pain I suffered for the heartless moon
Ended in bliss.
My eyes live on his face.

Lift up my dress, fill it with gold,
Yet never will I let him go again.
He is my shelter in the rains,
Ferry boat on the river.
He is my warmth when the winter is hard,
Cool breeze in the summer months.
Nothing else I need.

'The heartless moon' is, of course, Krishna.

The meaning is that however much she may be paid or given, she will never let Krishna go again.

NIGHT OF LOVE

A fateful night I spent,
Gazing at the moon
Like the face of my love.
Now are my life and youth fulfilled.
The air about me is free.
Home is home,
My body is my body.
My god is kind to me.
All doubts are gone.
Kokila, you may sing a million times,
A million moons may shine now.
Love's five arrows may become a million spears.
The southern breeze may gently blow.
So long as he is close to me,
My body shines as mine.

'My god is kind to me', i.e. Krishna.

'My body is my body' in the sense that assured of Krishna's love, she is now fully herself; she can no longer be destroyed by doubts, anxieties or fears; she can withstand any of the conventional excitants—the song of the *kokilas*, moonlight, the south wind.

'The southern breeze' is the 'Malayan' breeze of Sanskrit, a breeze which comes from the sandal-wood trees of the South and is supposed to inflame desire.

Kāma Deva, the god of love, is analogous to Eros or Cupid. He is armed with a bow and five arrows, the bow being often made of sugar-cane, the bow-string of a line of bees, the arrows of lotus-flowers with stalks.

Epithets for Kāma Deva include 'the beautiful', 'the inflamer', 'the lustful', 'the desirous', 'the gay', 'the lamp of honey', 'the bewilderer', 'the crackling fire', 'the stalk of passion', 'the destroyer of peace'.

NIGHTS OF JOY

O friend:
How can you ask me
What I feel?
In talk, love always grows,
Is always new.
Since I was born
I've seen his beauty
With insatiate eyes.
His gentle voice
Brushed my ears.
Thrilled, I long for more.
Nights of spring
Passed in joy,
Yet still the game of love
Has new delights.
I've held him to my heart
A million ages,
Yet longing flares again.
A host of lovers,
Their love reduced to ashes,
Know nothing of its power. . . .

Rādhā describing to a friend or confidante her love for Krishna.

TWIN HILLS

Her hair dense as darkness,
Her face rich as the full moon:
Unbelievable contrasts
Couched in a seat of love.
Her eyes rival lotuses.
Seeing that girl today,
My eager heart
Is driven by desire.

Innocence and beauty
Adore her fair skin.
Her gold necklace
Is lightning
On the twin hills,
Her breasts. . . .

SCARRED MOON

I cannot guess your heart,
O Mādhava.
The treasures of another man
I offered to you:
I was wrong
To bring a she-elephant to a lion.
Relinquish then the wife of another.

Your kisses have wiped clean
The mascara of her eyes.
Her lips are torn by your teeth.
Her full-grown breasts
Are scarred by your nails:
The autumn moon is scratched by Siva's peak. . . .

A maid or go-between addresses Krishna.

Following normal Indian usage, Rādhā is referred to as a 'she-elephant'—the extreme delicacy and grace of an elephant's movements impressing Indians far more than its bulk. The lion is, of course, Krishna.

The maid was 'wrong' to bring them together since not only would it be supremely difficult to steal or kidnap an elephant (and hence she was taking an unjustifiable risk) but as Rādhā was a married woman and, in fact, of a different caste from Krishna, the maid was also mixing two species (Krishna was born into the Yadava caste and was only *reared* by the cowherds).

The second verse gives another reason why the maid was 'wrong'. Krishna is a 'lion' not only because of his fierce love-making but because of the reckless daring with which he has left so many tell-tale marks on Rādhā's body.

'The autumn moon is scratched by Siva's peak.' Siva's peak (or crest) is Kailāsa, a mountain in the Himalayas. As the moon rises or sets behind the mountain, it is 'scratched' by its icy ridges. The moon is Rādhā's breasts, the peak Krishna's nails.

NIGHT OF RAIN

How the rain falls
In deadly darkness!
O gentle girl, the rain
Pours on your path
And roaming spirits straddle the wet night.
She is afraid
Of loving for the first time.
O Mādhava,
Cover her with sweetness.

How will she cross the fearful river
In her path?
Enraptured with love,
Beloved Rādhā is careless of the rest.

Knowing so much,
O shameless one,
How can you be cold towards her?
Whoever saw
Honey fly to the bee?

THE SEASON OF LOVE

Here is love
And there is fragrance.
There the mangoes are in bloom.
Here *kokilas*
Are singing in the fifth.
The season is ripe.
Bees float on the air,
Inhaling pollen,
Sucking honey.
The god of love
Is secretly setting
Flower-arrows to his bow. . . .

'Here *kokilas*
Are singing in the fifth.'

Each note in the Indian octave is derived from the cry or call of an animal or bird—the fifth note being supposedly modelled on the cry of the *kokila*, the first on that of a peacock, and so on.

HONEY IS LIFE

In the midst of thorns
Blossom flowers.
The foiled bee
Is wild with rage.
O Mālati,
My white fragrant flower,
Watching you,
Over and over again,
He longs to drink.
The anxious bee
Floats from spot to spot.
Away from you
He knows no rest.
Honey is his life.

O Mālati,
My ocean of honey,
Are you not ashamed to hoard it?
Whom can you blame for his death
If you are the murderer?

'Thorns' are a symbol for the lover's difficulties.

'Mālati' or jasmine is both a symbol for a lovely girl and a means of adorning the hair.

> Maids decorate their mass of curly hair
> Dark like the rain-cloud,
> With the fresh buds of the trailing *mālati*.
>
> (KĀLIDĀSA, *The Seasons*)

AS THE AUTUMN MOON

The darkness of separation is over.
Your face glows as the autumn moon.
Raise your eyes, O lovely darling,
Listen to my words,
This is no time for shyness.

O Mālati,
My flower of fragrant honey,
Your lover is here.
Let the bee take
His fill of sweetness.
King of the season,
Spring, too, is here.
Fulfil your promise. . . .

13.   MOONS AND MOONS (29, 43)

14.   'THINNER THAN THE CRESCENT' (35, 41)

15. 'HAIR DENSE AS DARKNESS' (16, 67)

16. THE GOD OF LOVE (19, 58, 64, 89)

17. 'BIND ME IN YOUR ARMS' (5, 14, 48)

NIGHT OF SPRING

Flowers in groves
Flutter at the birds' song.
Bees hum
And elephants trumpet.
On this night of spring,
Beautiful girl,
Abandon anger.
Does your heart ache?
Is your life gone far away?
As death's agent, the moon shines
For women parted from their lovers.
More delicate than a lotus
How can their fragile forms
Endure such pain?
Hot grows the fragrant sandal paste.
Hot the cool *kunda* flower.
Hot is the moon
And your necklace of polished pearls.
You cannot sleep
Though cool flowers
Cushion your sweet bed.
Your hair dishevelled,
Your clothes unmanageable,
Brood, then, on your lord of love.

'Flowers in groves
Flutter at the birds' song',

but, more literally, 'the vibrations set up by the birds' song are so
intense that they make the flowers in the grove shake'.

The 'anger' is, of course, feigned. The meaning is 'On this night of
spring, do not be stand-offish, let yourself go, don't pretend'.

FEVER OF LOVE

Tell me what to do.
Even the bed of water-drenched lotuses
Dries up as he reclines.
The coolness of sandal paste
Is no remedy,
Nor the hostile moon.

Be sure, O beautiful one,
Krishna pines away
From wanting you.
Day by day his body grows thin.
His heart ignores all others.
The doctors have left him
Without hope,
His only medicine
The nectar of your lips.

The moon is hostile since its very beauty, by reminding Rādhā of Krishna, provokes 'memory and desire', and thus inflames her fever.

A BED OF FLOWERS

A bed of flowers,
A glowing lamp
And scented sandal wood
Await you.
Whenever you were with her
To no avail time passed.
She stayed
Tortured by love.
O Mādhava,
Rādhā has made
Her love-bed for you . . .
O go to your tryst
At the waving flames
Of the forest-fire. . . .

'The forest fire', a fire but also a 'sympathetic setting'.

WAITING

He is happy, waiting
Waiting the whole night.
He never goes to bed.
Whoever comes
Appears to be you.
The forests and the gardens,
The groves and the huts
Are filled with your presence.
Again and again he swoons
Without you.
Such is his love.
O Mālati,
Sweet is your fate.

Lost without you,
He roams the earth.
The bee is possessed.
Jātaki and *ketaki*,
There are so many flowers
Yet their honey tastes the same.
Even in dreams he can look at none.
How can he devour their honey?
The heart returns to its snare.
Who can bind water
In its downward flow?

As in poem 20, Mālati is a jasmine flower but also a synonym for
Rādhā.

    Jātaki is an attractive wild flower, *ketaki*, the screw pine (*Pandanus
odoratissimus*; Hindi, *kevda*).

18.   BRANCHES AND FLOWERS (24, 31, 75)

19.

21.

20. 'THE BEE GOES TO HIS LOVE' (50)

19. 'THE NIGHT GREW AND ALL
WAS DONE' (66, 68, 72)

21. 'I BENT MY HEAD (80)

THE DEMON MOON

If I go I lose my home,
If I stay I lose my love . . .
The enemy moon
Wickedly bars my way.
The sky is bright from end to end.
Thinking it was dark,
I set out on my way
And then it rose
In its provoking form.
Who can control the demon moon?
But I must keep my tryst
With Krishna.

'The enemy moon', enemy because moonlight will reveal the lovers going to their tryst.

BLACK STONE

Your glances tempt their love ...
O Krishna, Krishna,
You are known to be wise.
How can I tell you what is right?

Gold is tested on the black-stone,
The love of a man by his nature.
Fragrance reveals the flower and its pollen
And the eyes and the tears
The dawn of love.

Kasauti, a black stone on which gold is rubbed and tested.

TIME AND LOVE

As I guard my honour,
My love in a foreign land
Ravishes beauties
Who belong to others.
Safely he will come,
But he has left me dead.
O traveller, tell him
That my youth wastes away . . .
If time goes on
Life too will go
And never shall we love again. . . .

'Ravishes beauties who belong to others.' Krishna, away from Rādhā, is enjoying other married women.

MOON AND NIGHT

When the moon is up,
O moon-faced love,
The rays from you both
Shine all around.
Your walk has the grace
Of the gait of an elephant.
Come to the tryst
While darkness is thick.

O moon-faced love,
The night is alight.
The fragrance of your skin
Floats free in the air.
From afar, the unkind
Can gaze at will.
How can I bring you there, my love?

Your eyes look everywhere.
Your body is afraid.
I dare not bring you.

The two greatest threats to illicit love are gossip and scandal. Anyone connected with a girl is only too anxious to besmear her reputation. Her greatest enemies are 'friends' and relatives. Hence, the poet says, the extreme need for caution, and the hazards of trysts on moonlit nights.

'The rays from you both'—the moon and Rādhā.

22. NIGHT OF SPRING (48, 56)

23. 'HER PAINTED FEET' (60)

24. GONE AWAY LOVE (31, 49

25. 'FRAGRANCE OF FLOWERS'

MOUNTAINS OF GOLD

In joyous words he spoke
Of the beauty of my face.
Thrilled, my body
Glowed and glowed.
My eyes that watched love spring
Were wet with joy.
In dream tonight
I met the king of honey . . .
He seized the end of my dress,
The strings broke loose
With all the weight of love.
My hands leapt to my breasts
But the petals of lotus could not hide
The mountains of gold.

'Mountains of gold', the breasts; 'petals of lotus', the hands.

GONE AWAY LOVE

Hearing the signal,
She went to the tryst
But you were gone.
The shape of beauty
Longed to hear your voice
But in despair
The night dissolved. . . .

THE END OF YOUTH

I hide my shabby cheeks
With locks of hair,
And my grey hairs
In folds of flowers.
I paint my eyes
With black mascara.
The more I try
The more absurd I look.
My breasts loosely dangle.
My curving lines are gone.
My youth is ended
And love roams wild
In all my skin and bones.
O sadness, my sadness,
Where is my youth?

Lament by an ageing woman; or perhaps Rādhā brooding on her dire future.

REMEMBERED LOVE

Harder than diamonds,
Richer than gold,
Deeper than the sea
Was our love.
The sea still washes the shores
But our love went dry.
I wish my lover,
Who is dark as the clouds,
Would come in torrents. . . .

How I remember
Those hours of passion
When he would swear to me
That day was night. . . .

'Dark as the clouds' is Rādhā recalling Krishna. For a discussion of Krishna's dark skin, see *The Loves of Krishna*.

GRIEF

Her flowing tears
Made pools at her feet.
The lotus that grew on the land
Now floats on water.
Her lips have lost their colour,
Like new leaves bitten by frost. . . .

Rādhā is grieving for her lost love.

THINNER THAN THE CRESCENT

Her tears carved a river
And she broods on its bank,
Hurt and confused.
You ask her one thing,
She speaks of another.
Her friends believe
That joy may come again.
At times they banish hope
And cease to care.

O Mādhava,
I have run to call you.
Rādhā each day
Grows thinner,
Thinner than the crescent in the sky. . . .

Rādhā pining in Krishna's absence.

LET NO ONE BE A GIRL

Let no one be born,
But if one must
Let no one be a girl.
If one must be a girl
Then may she never fall in love,
If she must fall in love,
Free her from her family.
O make me sure of him until I end.

Should I meet my lover
And his love flow strongly
Like currents of a river,
Let his darling heart
Be free of other girls.
If he yields to other loves,
Let him know his mind and heart. . . .

'Free her from her family'; save her from the taunts of her family and their inquisitive supervision.

'Let him know his mind and heart.' Let him, at least, know what he is doing and realize the anguish he is causing.

FEAR

My shyness left me
As he looted my clothes.
My lover's limbs became my dress.
Like a bee
Hovering on a lotus bud,
He lent across the lamp.

The god of love is never shy.
He brightens like the bird
That loves the clouds.
Yet still as I remember
My darling's wild tricks,
My heart, shyly trembling,
Is bruised with fear.

The *chataka* or hawk-cuckoo (*Hierococcyx varius*) is believed to live on rain-water and hence to 'brighten' at the sight of clouds.

26. NIGHT OF STORM (64, 71, 86, 87)

27. 'YET STILL AS I REMEMBER' (37)

A DARK DAY

A dark day
The cloud broke,
Rain fell.
I dressed for my love,
Believing it was night.
My deed of daring
Brought us to our goal.
The cloud
Kept other eyes away.
O friend,
How can I tell you what I felt?
To steal an elephant in broad daylight. . . .

For a girl to meet her lover by day and not be seen or caught is as difficult as stealing an elephant in broad daylight.

PURSUED

My eyes pursued
That lovely Rādhā
The whole long way. . . .

Her sweet nature lit her face
Her eyelids fluttered
Below her curving brows.
Her eyes, like bees
On a lotus sucking honey,
Spread their wings to fly.

Today I saw her going.
Her beauty stayed,
Tied to my heart.
My heart, her beauty,
Rushed to the valley
Of two golden hills.
The god of love
Elected to punish me
And held me captive
In the hills of her breasts.

The punishment which is no punishment.

MY BODY HID MY BODY

My eyes encountered him
And left me.
The lotus snubbed the sun
And fled away.
The moon and the night-lily
Unite in love.
Mādhava I saw today,
But with art I hid my passion.

Shyness dropped with my clothes.
My body hid my body.
My heart was another's.
Krishna I saw
Everywhere.

'The lotus snubbed the sun.' Rādhā, dazed by Krishna, avoids his eyes.

> 'The moon and the night-lily
> Unite in love.'

Rādhā's hand (the night-lily) covers up her face (the moon).

The meaning is that she was so absorbed in Krishna that although her clothes slipped down, she did not realize that she was naked. 'My body hid my body' 'My heart was another's'. She felt, in fact, as if she were no longer there.

SORROW

Clouds filled the sky
And the god of love,
Piercing her heart, withdrew.
Leaning on the ground
She lifts her frail form. . . .

O Krishna,
Cast aside your moods . . .
Like the dimmed moon
In a dark fortnight
Rādhā fades.
Is she an evening star?
Is she the pale crescent moon
Of the wet monsoon sky?
Krishna, you have turned your face away,
Inflicting pain unbearable.

8. THE DEMON MOON (26, 29, 49, 63)

29. 'GOLDEN PITCHERS' (5)

ECSTASY

Her hair, dishevelled,
Veils the beauty of her face
As evil shadows eat the glowing moon.
Strings of blossom in her hair
Wantonly play
As flooded rivers
Twine about their twins.

Exquisite today,
This sport of love,
As Rādhā rides on Krishna.
Beads of sweat glisten on her face
Like pearls on the moon,
A present to her
From the god of love.

With all her force
She kisses her lover's lips,
Like the moon swooping
To drink a lotus bloom.
Her necklace dangles
Below her hanging breasts,
Like streams of milk
Trickling from golden jars.
The jingling bells around her waist
Sang glory to the god of love.

'As flooded rivers
Twine about their twins.'

Rivers that normally run parallel to each other get merged together
at times of flood.

'Rādhā rides on Krishna' is a reference to Rādhā's active role
at the climax of their love-making.

MOONS AND MOONS

There is the one and only moon,
And then the moon
That haloes the crown of Siva.
There are people with the name 'Moon'.

I saw one moon in the sky
But there were three with you.
That exquisite sight of the night
Confused my heart.

Who could believe
That there are moons and moons,
Held in a single place?

Which is the moon of the stars
And which the moon among girls,
And which moon shines
On the feathers of the night birds?

One moon plays with Mādhava
And another in the sky.

'But there were three with you.' Rādhā's three moons are, of course, her face and breasts.

'Night birds' are *chakoras* (*Alectoris Graeca*), a kind of partridge, supposed to dote on the moon.

ANGUISH

When the moon-face, brooding,
Gleams in her hands,
New leaves caress
The lotus bud.
What can that lotus-face say?
It is not she
Who is to blame
When Krishna harshly turned aside.
Streams of tears
Glitter in her eyes
Like a dark bird
That vomits pearls.

The ache of parting
Has thinned her body.
The flower has withered
But the fragrance stays.
Anguish eats her life
Yet still
The arrows of love
Strike hard.

'New leaves caress
The lotus bud.'

Rādhā hides her face between her fingers.
'Like a dark bird
That vomits pearls', or more literally, like the *khanjaria*, a kind of
black wagtail (*Montacilla Alba*) which having swallowed some
pearls vomits them.

HILLS OF GOLD

Your eyes are tired and red
Like birds drugged with moonshine
And your eye-brows,
Tense and still,
Are like the bows
Of the god of love
Left after battle.
Do not pretend, O darling Rādhā.
Words hide, acts speak.

Your lovely breasts
Seem like hills of gold,
Scarred with blossom.
Your curls are gone,
Your tresses tangled
And the god of love
Smiles at your disarray.

'Birds drugged with moonshine', *chakoras* (Poem 43).

'Your eye-brows tense and still.'

When in use, a bow-string quivers and is constantly moving. When no longer required (i.e. when the battle is over), it remains stiff and rigid. Similarly, after loving a whole night, Rādhā is so exhausted that she cannot even move her eye-brows.

> 'Your lovely breasts
> Seem like hills of gold,
> Scarred with blossom',

scarred because of the scratches given by Krishna's nails. Scratch marks on the breasts are compared to blossom on hills.

30. 'STALWART AS A TREE HIS DEEP EMBRACE' (48)

31.   THE AGONY OF LOVE (10, 22)

THE RAGE OF LOVE

The more that gold
Is purified by fire,
The richer it becomes.
The more a lover
Is moved to anger,
The better is he
For the role of love.
O darling love,
Let violent moods not sway your heart.
Roused by love,
If your lover utters words,
It is not his fault.
Often has he promised
And often failed.
He is not made
Without flesh and blood
Nor is he a snake
That lives on air.

To a lover a constant anxiety is lest he should fail to reach an expected ideal. If he 'disappoints', he easily becomes annoyed, has 'moods' or gets tense and irritable. The woman, the poet argues, should realize that this is the price she must pay for her lover's ardour.

APPROACH OF SPRING

Let us watch
The spring appear
When the white *kundas* bloom
In majestic smiles.
The brilliant moon
Floats as a lover bee.
Bright is the night
And darkness shrouds the day.
Enchanted girls
Spurn love in pride
And the god of love
Leers like an enemy.

Spring is the time for love. Night and day, therefore, cannot and should not be distinguished.

The purpose of the god of love is to see that women yield themselves to their lovers. Any reluctance on their part (whether real or feigned) is thus an affront—to be treated by him as a declaration of war. He will then 'leer like an enemy' and desist only when their pride has been destroyed.

THE FOREST OF LOVE

Stalwart as a tree,
His deep embrace
Squeezes the vine
With branch-like arms.
When I want to sleep,
Krishna makes love
The whole night through,
Like a bee that lingers
On the fragrant *mālati*.
He sucks my lips.
The forest has burst open
With white *kunda* blooms,
But the bee is enraptured
By *mālati* and her honey.

Of the two jasmines, *mālati* and *kunda*, *mālati* (Rādhā) is the more fragrant and hence is preferred by the bee (Krishna).

SAD LOVE

The moon spits fire,
Lotuses droop
And loaded with fragrance
Mingle in sad love.
Kokila, bird of spring,
Why do you torture?
Why do you sing
Your love-provoking song?
My lover is not here
And yet the god of love
Schemes on and on.
You do not know the meaning of 'tomorrow'.
'Tomorrow' is *my* tomorrow
And water
Escapes the dam of youth.
You are in love,
So is your lover,
And your two banks
Are brimming with the flood.
My lover left and I would die
Than wait still longer
For his loved return.
The fragrance of flowers
Enters the city,
Bees sing,
The moon and night enchant,
Yet all are enemies.

Bemoaning her separation from Krishna, Rādhā upbraids the god of love for arousing in her such keen desires. 'You' is a female *kokila* bird, happily mated. The flowers, bees and moonlight are 'enemies' since, instead of enhancing Rādhā's joy, they kindle passion without assuaging it.

SMILES AND LAUGHTER

Blue lotuses
Flower everywhere
And black *kokilas* sing . . .
King of the seasons,
Spring has come
And wild with longing
The bee goes to his love.
Birds flight in the air
And cowherd-girls
Smile face to face . . .
Krishna has entered
The great forest.

Compare Shakespeare (*As You Like It*)

In spring time,
The only pretty ring time,
When birds do sing,
Hey ding a ding, ding:
Sweet lovers love the spring.

INDIFFERENCE

At first you made our eyes meet,
Then you gave me hope,
Glancing and smiling.
Yet now you seem
Indifferent
To your promise.
O my sweet darling,
What happened to your love?
Have you then wiped away
Our first kiss? . . .

This is not, as we might at first suppose, a lover addressing his
mistress, but Rādhā upbraiding Krishna.

NEW LOVE

Style of the new moon, stirrings of new love,
Scratches of nails scarring her firm breasts.
At times she eyes them and at times she shields,
As poor hands cover treasure dear as life.
For the first time she knew the act of love.
The joys of dalliance fill her thoughts,
Wrapping her round with shudderings of delight.
Safe from the eyes of vicious friends,
She holds a gem as mirror to her face,
Lowers her brow that none can see
And then with tender care
Studies the love-bites on her lower lip.

'Vicious friends.' As in other poems, 'friends' play a somewhat ambivalent role. The supposed 'friend' is often inquisitive, eaten up with curiosity and ready to betray the most private confidences. At the same time, she provides comfort, gives sympathy and under-standing and often sustains morale.

STOLEN LOVE

The lotus blooms
For those who can admire.
The thirsty bee takes pollen.
Moons of nipples
Show thick scars of nails.
The bird of spring
Chuckles as he sees.
O proud darling,
Turn your head and look.
The scarlet dawn
Drinks darkness of the night.
Proud one,
Your honour is your wealth.
My theft of it was wrong
And for this crime
The god of love
Has seized my heart
And holds it in strict charge.

We may take this poem in two senses. In a first view, the lover has visited his mistress, counting on again spending the whole night locked in her arms. The visit, however, has been a failure. He has either wooed her poorly or she has not been 'in the mood'. They have not made love and now it is too late. The dawn has come. He asks forgiveness for having enjoyed her previously and declares that, as a punishment, the god of love 'has seized his heart' and 'holds it in strict charge'.

In a second view, they have in fact made love. The lady, however, has had second thoughts and instead of delighting in the lover's presence, is now inclined to regret her rapid surrender. Confronted by what the Sanskrit poet, Amaru, terms 'the disease of sulking', the lover can only admit his fault, urge the strength of her charms and blame the god of love.

COUNTERFEIT

When you stay before my eyes
You make me feel your love is firm,
But out of sight how different you are!
How long does false gold shine?
Master of sweetness, I know your ways.
Your heart is counterfeit.
Your love is words.
Speech, love and humour
All are smooth
And only meant to tease.
When you shed a girl,
Do you laugh?
Are your arrows always
Poisoned with honey?

Krishna is shown as the smooth and facile charmer.

FIRST JOY

Away with childish thoughts.
Come to the bed.
Give up your shyness.
Lift your face.
Why waste time
Scratching lines on the earth?

O beautiful Rādhā,
Stay with your lover.
Brush aside your fear.
For the first time
Join with him in love.

Your first joy
May soon become
Love's own great play
Of the lotus and the bee. . . .

SPOILT LOVE

The sun rose
On the shores of the lake.
The wind was cool as dew.
I was tired from making love.
O friend, my night of spring
Was spoilt by sleep.
Cruel it was of Krishna
To go away
Without a word.
If only he had spoken,
I would have given him
A fond embrace
Like waves surging
On a stony shore.
The more I dwell
On all my passionate thoughts,
Sadness unspeakable
Drains my lonely love. . . .

Rādhā is distraught lest her tiredness has exasperated Krishna and made him leave her. Now that he has gone away, without a word, she does not know how to find him or how to make a new tryst.

LOVE AND YOUTH

In those few days
Sparkling with youth,
Mādhava adored me.
Now the flower
Has lost its scent.
No one cares
For a dried-up lake. . . .

Rādhā bemoans her fading charms.

FIRE

Birds of spring,
Black *kokilas*,
Loudly call on every side.
Bees run wild.
No one cares for guarded treasures.
Love is let loose,
He is roaming and looting
The pride of the girls.
O friend, I cannot understand my fate
To be so pestered by the god of love.
New leaves freshen mangoes
Like flags of welcome fluttering on the gates.
Arrows of flowers
Fly from the taut bow
And I am tortured.
Who said
The southern breeze was soothing?
Its gentle touch kills lonely women
And the pollen of flowers
Scorches like a fire.

'Guarded treasures' are, of course, girls ripe for love.

'Arrows of flowers' are the arrows of Kāma Deva, the god of love.

In mediaeval India it was the custom to adorn the gates of a town with banners—to 'put out the flags'—for visiting dignitaries. The mangoes with their new leaves—another sign of spring—are compared to gates bedecked with flags.

NEGLECT

Has then my lover been suborned by others?
Has he succumbed to yet another girl
Who also knows the ways of love?
What evil course has turned the gods against me
That Krishna never even says my name?
O friend, tell me what to do.
He lives in the same village
Yet might be in another land.
The god of love lassoes me with hope.
Only with death do girls abandon longing.
O when will end these days of waiting?
Youth is unstable, life so short.

Rādhā mourns Krishna's neglect.

THE RIVAL

The lamp-black of her eyes
Is stolen by your lips
And her lips' red
Rouges your eyes.
O do not hide your face,
Putting me off with silly lies.
O Mādhava,
Let us not talk
Of your behaviour now.
Go to the tryst,
To the company
Of that enchanting girl
With whom you spent the night.
Most fortunate of all
Girls in Gokula,
How can I appraise her luck?
Her painted feet
Left foot-prints on your chest,
Telling the tale of all your love.

'Lamp-black' is collyrium or kohl, used like mascara for blackening the eyelids and thus enhancing the eyes' charm. The black marks on Krishna's mouth convince Rādhā that he has spent the night with another of the cowgirls.

Feet were painted red with henna, like toe or nail varnish.

'Gokula.' The village in the Brindaban forest where Krishna dwelt with the cowherds.

EMPTY HOUSE

Roaring the clouds break
And rain falls.
The earth becomes a sea.
In a far land, my darling
Can think of nothing
But his latest love.
I do not think
That he will now return.
The god of love rejects me.
A night of rain,
An empty house
And I a woman and alone.
The streams grow to great rivers.
The fields lie deep in water.
Travellers cannot now reach home.
To all, the ways are barred.
May that god without a body
Strip me of my body too.

Says Vidyāpati:
When he remembers, Krishna will return.

The 'far land' is Mathura, a day's march from Gokula. When Krishna goes to Mathura to accomplish his destiny and rid the world of the tyrant Kansa, Rādhā and the cowgirls assume that some of the Mathura women, the 'city girls', will ensnare him and thus delay or prevent his return.

In the *Bhāgavata Purāna*, the classic text of the tenth century, Krishna leaves for Mathura and never returns. In the later cult of Rādhā and Krishna, on the other hand, his departure for Mathura, and subsequent wanderings, are only minor episodes in the main romance. Krishna leaves Rādhā *in order to return* and all his later life (as feudal magnate, married to Rukmini) is disregarded.

'The bodiless' is another synonym for Kāma Deva, the god of love—perhaps referring to his encounter with Siva, when a glance from the latter's third eye reduced him to ashes.

DENIAL

Seeing the bright moon
Betray the path,
She bent her face
And cried aloud.
She took mascara from her eyes
And painted Rāhu
Eating the moon.
O Mādhava,
In a foreign land
Harsh is the heart.
Come back.
I have seen your loved one
Frightened of the god of love.
She calls on Siva
Again and again,
Writhing in the dust,
Offering
Her breasts and hands.
Her body once clutched by your fingers,
She cannot bear the southern breeze.
Gone is her life yet hope teases her
And still she plays
With the fangs of a snake.

Rāhu is a demon who is supposed to eat the sun and moon, thus causing an eclipse. Painting 'Rāhu eating the moon' is a form of sympathetic magic designed to bring on darkness and thus enable her to keep the tryst.

Siva is Rādhā's 'God' on whom she calls in time of trouble. Fruits and flowers are tendered in worship. Not having any with her, Rādhā offers Siva her breasts (in place of the customary *bel* fruits, round and sunny like grape-fruits and Siva's favourite fruit). She gives him her 'hands' in place of lotuses.

WATCHING EYES

Pull up your anklets.
Muffle the jingling girdle
With your hands
And walking on the path,
Mingle your body with the dark.
For soon the demon moon will rise
To watch the joys of love,
The lotus blooming in delight.
Quick, quick, O lovely face,
For naughty eyes like thirsty birds
Float all about you.
O Rādhā, why did you adorn your hair
And use a tell-tale unguent on your skin?
You are in love
And so is your lover
And all the world will know it. . . .

Even at night there are watching eyes, drinking in the scene.
'Thirsty birds' are *chakoras* panting for moonlight.

THICK NIGHT

Nocturnal spirits are abroad.
Fierce snakes
Wander in darkness
And only lightning
Lifts the gloom.
Through the thick night
You bravely go.
O friend,
Who is that treasure among men
Who stole your heart,
To whom you hurry
Eager to be loved?
Before you flows the Jamnā
Fraught with perils
And you must cross its dreaded stream
To offer him your joys.
Beside you goes the guardian god
Armed with flower-arrows.
Have no fear and yet
I tremble for you.

The Jamnā, a great river of northern India, adjoins Brindaban,
the haunt of Krishna, Rādhā and the cowgirls. In Krishna's youth,
it was infested by a giant snake, Kāliya, whose poison fouled its
waters. On one occasion, Krishna leapt into the river, subdued the
snake but spared it on condition that it left the river and troubled
the cowherds no more. 'Dreaded stream' may either refer to the
snake or the river's treacherous currents.

'The guardian god' is Kāma Deva, god of love, at whose instance
Rādhā is going to the tryst.

CLOUD

Cloud,
King of the waters,
I am a *chataka* bird
That lives on rain.
Give me water,
Yet no rain comes
When most I need you.
Cloud,
Give me water,
Save my life. . . .

The cloud is Krishna, the *chataka* bird, Rādhā.

NEW TO LOVE

New to love,
I shrank from loving,
Yet the night grew
And all was done.
I did not relish
Sweets of dalliance.
My shyness warred against my will . . .
He seized my garland,
Held my hair
And pressed his heart
Against my smothered breasts
But, in my clumsy innocence,
Alone, with none to aid,
I could not please.
He wanted everything
In one great rapture
And to my painful shame
I gave so little.
The spell of passion went.
I said
Nothing.

Garlands of white flowers were worn by lovers. They would often get broken during love-making.

For a similar situation compare a verse by Amaru (trans. Basham):

Fool that I was, why didn't I clasp the lord of my life to my neck?
Why did I turn my face away when he wanted to kiss me?
Why did I not see? Why did I not speak? So, when love is first awakened,
A girl is filled with remorse as she thinks of her childish shyness.

FIRST LOVE

Asked for her lips,
She bows her head.
She cannot bear
His hands upon her breasts.
She tightly holds
Her loosened girdle,
As flushing skin
Betrays her mounting love.
Gentle the girl,
So skilled her lover—
How will they play
The game of passion?
Her breasts in bud
Still hidden in her palms,
The crisp green plums
That change to crimson red. . . .

His nails grow eager
To set upon her breasts,
Her eyebrows curving
Like the crescent moon.
Greedy for her face, he wonders
How long can the moon
Hide within her dress.

HONEY SWEET

As I near the bed,
He smiles and gazes.
Flower-arrows fill the world.
The sport of love,
Its glow and luxuries
Are indescribable, O friend,
And when I yield myself,
His joy is endless.

Freeing my skirt,
He snatches at my garland.
My downcast mind
Is freed of frontiers,
Though my life is held
In the net of his love.
He drinks my lips.
With heart so thrilled,
He takes my clothes away.
I lose my body
At his touch
And long to check
But grant his love.

Says Vidyāpati:
Sweet as honey
Is the talk of a girl in love.

THE LOTUS SMILED

... On all my limbs
Were spells of love.
What strength I needed
To arrest desire.
My quivering breasts
I hid with trembling hands
As all my body glowed.
No longer could I check my passion
And the shut lotus bloomed in smiles.

FLASH OF EYES

You have stolen the moon,
O lovely face,
Your honour is at stake.
Restrain your glances.
Let no one see you,
Lest Rāhu eat you
Mistaking you for the moon.
Your eyes flash
With black mascara,
Making glances
Sharp as arrows. . . .

You have stolen nectar.
You have stolen the moon . . .
But where will you put it
So brightly does it shine?

'Your honour is at stake.' By 'stealing the moon', or, in other words,
by having such a lovely face, she will attract countless admirers.

DARKNESS AND RAIN

Clouds break.
Arrows of water fall
Like the last blows
' That end the world.
The night is thick
With lamp-black for the eyes.
Who but you, O friend,
Would keep so late a tryst?
The earth is a pool of mud
With dreaded snakes at large.
Darkness is everywhere,
Save where your feet
Flash with lightning.

'The last blows that end the world' are the deluge which ends a world cycle.

'You' is Rādhā.

AFTERMATH

Your eyes droop with sleep
Yet still your face
Outshines the lotus.
Who was that fool
Who scarred your breasts,
Marring their god-like charms
With savage nails?
Your brow no longer wears
Its mark of scarlet.
Your lips of coral
Are drained grey.
Who has raided, my love,
Your house of treasure?

WEALTH OF YOUTH

On this earth
In wavering life
Youth is short-lived.
Enjoy it as you can
Or stab the heart.
O lovely girl,
Where is your wisdom?
The wealth of youth
Is yours
To be offered as a gift.
Give it as you will
It still remains.
Only he is poor
Whom you deny. . . .

In giving herself, the girl remains rich and, at the same time, enriches her lover. If she refuses him, it is the lover who stays poor.

WAXING MOON

Do not abandon
Her delicate limbs
For fear of crushing.
Who has ever seen
A blossom smothered
By the weight of a bee?
Mādhava, mark my words:
Do not hold back
If she cries 'No, no',
Or futile comes the dawn.
With your ardent kissing
Give her lips
The hue of dusk
And slowly bring her
To the height of joy.
The play of love,
Its keen delights,
Should grow and grow
Like the white brilliance
Of a waxing moon.

SHOOTS OF LOVE

In our two hearts
Those shoots of love
Opened with two or three leaves.
Then grew the branches
And the clusters of foliage.
They were covered with flowers
And scent lay everywhere.

But my love and hopes
Abruptly ended.
O friend,
Krishna, that charming cheat,
Will he ever return?

LOST LOVE

When growing love has gone,
The cheeks are smudged
With lamp-black from the eyes.
My body slumps in languor
And love tastes bitter as a gourd.
If you ask me, friend,
Chance is love's nature,
Fickleness my lover's;
But that others should know
Pricks me like a thorn.

The bird of spring,
The black *kokila*,
Fans the fire of parting
And Krishna provokes it
Sprinkling water.

By reminding Rādhā of herself Krishna provokes the fire of parting. When only a little water is put on a fire, instead of putting it out, it seems to make it burn the fiercer.

WAR OF YOUTH

Two armies were engaged in war
As childhood merged in youth.
Knotted, the hair of Rādhā fell.
At times, she hid her limbs,
At times, released their charm.
Her eyes in innocence roved here and there.
The skin about her rising breasts
Was tinged with red.
Her feet became
As restless as her heart.
The god was waking up in Rādhā.
His eyes were closed with love.

Although regarded as a god with bow and arrows, Kāma Deva, the god of love, was believed to dwell in lovers' bodies, infusing them with his own powers and thus becoming in a sense a god without a body. For this reason, as well as from his encounter with Siva, he is often referred to as 'the bodiless one'.

In Spring the bodiless Love permeates
The limbs of a maiden, in manifold ways;
Into the visionless eyes
He puts a sparkle and a softness;
He is the pallor of the cheeks,
And the hardness of the breasts;
He moulds the slimness of the hips,
It is love's beauty itself
That shines through her loveliness.

(KĀLIDĀSA, *The Seasons*)

STEPS AND MUSIC

On twin hills
The moon shone
And from a lotus bloom
Issued a pair of rays.
In scarlet flowers
Were chosen pearls.
Lovely that god's creation
Whose face I saw today.
Her curving thighs
Were like a plantain tree
Laden with lilies of the earth.
Her steps made music
To rouse the ruling god of love.

Each image is a symbol. 'Twin hills' are the breasts, 'the moon' and 'lotus bloom' the face, 'a pair of rays' the eyes, 'scarlet flowers' the lips, 'chosen pearls' the teeth.

WAVES OF LIGHTNING

Her feet showered lotuses.
The glitter of her body
Brought waves of lightning.
The enchanting beauty
Has entered my heart.
Her eyes opened
Like lotuses in flower.
Her widening smile
Cast nectar-spells on all.
Her sidelong glances
Issued darts of love.
I saw her beauty
Only in a flash
But thinking of it
Fills three different worlds.

The 'three different worlds' are heaven, earth and the nether regions.

STOLEN GLANCE

I bent my head
To stop my eyes from stealing,
Yet still they ran
To drink the face
Of my sweet love.
They ran like *chakora* birds
Soaring for the moon.
I forced them from his face
And pulled them to my feet.
Like bees drunk with honey
My eyes could scarcely fly,
Yet even then
They spread their wings.

Listening to Mādhava's sweet enchantments,
In ecstasy I closed my ears
And then the god of love
Lifted his bow
And sprayed me with his arrows.
My body was borne away
By the dew of my skin.
My make-up was afloat.
Trembling with delight,
My breasts burst from my bodice
And my bracelets were in pieces.

CARE

To all my sadness, friend,
There is no end.
From his flute, a breath of poison
Clouded my limbs,
Forcing its way
Into my ears,
Melting my pride, my heart.

Needles of delight
Pricked my body.
I dared not gaze at him
In such an older throng
With blaming eyes around.
Waves of love rose high.
I hid my limbs
In the folds of my dress
And toiled back home
With listless steps.

As a cowherd among cowherds, Krishna learnt to play the flute,
his flute-playing specially charming Rādhā and the cowgirls. Since
Rādhā was a married woman, she dared not gaze at Krishna in
public.

EYES OF DANGER

To gaze on Krishna was my greatest wish,
Yet seeing him was filled with danger.
Gazing has bewitched me, no will remains,
I cannot speak or hear.
Like monsoon clouds,
My eyes pour water.
My heart flutters.
O friend, why ever did I see him
And with such joy deliver him my life? . . .

INNOCENCE

Krishna, if you touch me by force,
The guilt of murder will be on your hands.
O master of love,
You are stubborn with experience.
I do not know whether
Love is bitter or sweet.
It makes me shudder
When I hear of love. . . .

Says Vidyāpati:
If I know the truth,
A fruit is not sweet when green.

A warning against making love to too young a girl.

TODAY

Leave my dress alone,
Dear love,
No wealth of passion
Is hidden by its knot.
Only today I heard
Of passionate joy
And do not know as yet
What joy it means.
Wherever I can
I shall search and search.
I shall ask my friends
If I have it in my home.
For once, O Mādhava,
Listen to my words:
Aided by friends,
I shall look for this joy
And when I find it, bring it you.

OCEAN OF NECTAR

Sweet girl,
So strange you seem today
And your eyes and your face
Look different.
As you speak,
You lose the thread of your thoughts.
Your lips turn pale.
Beloved in passion,
Who shared the joys of love with you?
Your secret is out, why are you so shy?
His forces of love
The god has roused in you.
Your thighs tremble.
The golden skin of your breasts
Is scarlet from his nails
Yet still you try to hide them.

Rādhā, you are an ocean of nectar
And Krishna is afloat in it
Like a furious elephant.

The poet addresses Rādhā.

THE NIGHT'S STONE

Mādhava:
In many ways
Your sweet love goes.
She tried the gold of love
On a black monsoon night,
A night that was her testing stone.
Clouds roared in the sky
But she did not care.
Lightning flashed
But she did not turn.
The frightened world
Watched the rain pour down,
Washing the darkness—
Colour of kohl.
Dancing on the hoods
Of fleeing snakes,
She covered with her hands
Their glittering heads.
She kissed the water-laden clouds
As nearer came her meeting.

For a girl to go to her lover on a night of storm is like testing gold
on a stone.

CLOUDS AND LIGHTNING

Love, sweet love,
Come to the tryst.
The day is good
In the kingdom of love
The king is spreading his spells.
The elders are blinded.
Darkness covers friends.
Come, sweet love,
Come to the tryst.
Your breasts are twitching
With auspicious signs.
Carry your faith,
Your will and fear
To the temple of the lord.
May the tree of your wish
Be laden with fruit,
For ever enchanted
By your dearest's love.

Clouds with lightning,
Lightning with the clouds
Whisper and roar.
Branches in blossom
Shower in joy
And peacocks loudly chant
For both of you.

BOLD LOVE

I am going today, dear friend,
And shall not fear the elders at home.
Words will not trouble me.
With sandal paste my skin will glisten.
I shall deck myself in pearls.
My eyes look brilliant with no mascara.
I shall cover my body in white
And walk with leisured steps.
When the sky is lit with the smiling moon
From staring eyes I shall not flinch
Nor shall I hide.
So much did I conceal
From fear of others,
Even the currents of my love.

THE ROBBER

I was alone. My friends had gone ahead. The night was dark and lightning flashed.

As I came from the grove, he stopped. Only Krishna would have dared to plunder me. The world would have blamed me if he had taken away my clothes.

'Leave my dress alone, Krishna,' I cried; 'it is new and you will tear it.'

HEAT

The heat of the sun
Sets the earth ablaze.
The sand burns.
Desire mounts . . .
On lotus-soft feet
The lovely girl,
At the dawn of her youth,
Makes for the tryst. . . .

CHASING THE DAY

O friend:
My love has still not come.
His heart is hard as thunder.
I have worn out my finger-tips,
Tracing the day of his return.
I have dimmed my eyes
Scanning his path. . . .

He left me so young.
Now I am ripe
For words of love
He dwells with me no more.
My sweet love promised to return. . . .

MASTER OF LOVE

My Krishna is so very clever.
With no effort on his part,
He broke my all-resisting pride.
Today he came garbed as a *yogi*
To mystify me by an exquisite act . . .
But he was overwhelmed at seeing my face.
When he begged the jewel of my pride,
I knew how cunning was his mind.
And then what he said
I am too shy to repeat.
No one even knew
That this was the master of love.

Yogis are Hindu ascetics who often wear saffron robes.

SPRING AND LOVE

The trees grow again. Fresh flowers bloom. The spring comes with the fragrant southern wind and bees are drunk. The forest of Brinda is filled with new airs.

Krishna has come.

On the river bank adorned with groves, new lovers are lost in love. Intoxicated by the honey of mango blossoms, *kokilas* freshly sing. The hearts of young girls are drunken with delight.

The forest is charged with a new flavour of love. . . .

Compare John Gay, *The Beggars' Opera*.

> Youth's the season made for joys,
> Love is then our duty.
> She alone who that employs
> Well deserves her beauty.
> Let's be gay
> While we may,
> Beauty's a flower
> Despised in decay.
>
> . . . .
>
> Dance and sing,
> Time's on the wing:
> Life never knows
> The return of spring.

THE BOAT

On sharp currents of the river
The boat was launched.
But Krishna was young,
He could not steer it.
So I swam across.
My bracelets snapped,
My necklace broke.
Friend, O friend,
Do not scold me with harsh words.
My ear-rings dropped in the river.
I searched for them till dusk.
My make-up was washed away.
My face looks clean as the moon.
Idling on the banks of the river,
My breasts were scratched with thorns.

Says Vidyāpati:
You talk so plausibly,
People might even believe you.

The theme of the alibi or 'false excuse' occurs also in popular Indian poetry.

THE QUEST

So long our world was new,
We were one like fish and water.
Such was our love.
A sharp word passed between us.
My dear love smiled
And gave no answer.
Krishna, in the same bed with me,
Seemed in a far-away land.
In the forest where no one moves,
My love now smiles,
My love now speaks.
I shall dress as a *yogini*
And look for my love.

A *yogini* is a female ascetic.

THE DANCE

Young girls are dancing.
They are no longer shy.
The king-dealer in love,
The spring, has come.
The slender and tall,
They all have come,
Dressed in different ways.
Some wear silk
With garlands on their necks.
Others are made up
With scented sandal paste.
Their breath is perfumed.
Some have bodies
Golden with saffron.
Others have raised
Tiers of pearls on their hair.

TIME OF LOVE

Tender, beautiful
Are the new leaves.
The forest is wrapped in red.
The southern breeze sways,
Drunk with its scent of blossom.
The spring has opened in Brindaban
And Krishna heralds joy.
Kokilas call from the mango blooms
For the new power reigning the earth,
The god of love.
The messenger bees were drinking honey
Wandering, watching for women of pride.
In the forest Krishna was busy
Enclosed in the round dance.

'Women of pride' are those whose seduction will be slow and difficult, yet when accomplished infinitely rewarding; or, in the alternative, those who privately want advances, but publicly discourage them.

'Women of pride' are singled out for the love-god's attentions since their mastery is all the more gratifying.

THE SEASON OF HONEY

The season of honey
Enters sweet Brindaban.
The bees drunk wild
With sweet blossom's honey
Float row upon row.
Sweeter still are the lord of love
And the sporting honey-girls.
Sweetness and delight
Blend with the flavour of art.
Instruments ring.
Sweet cymbals crash
As the honey-girls move
With their partners in the dance.
Honeyed steps follow
The songs of sweet delight.

AT THE RIVER

Hold my hand.
Caress me, Krishna.
I will give you
A wondrous garland.
The friends are gone,
But which way, Krishna,
I do not know.
I will not walk
With you, Krishna,
But at the river
By the lonely bank
There I will meet you.

PARTED LOVE

I could not suffer the least delay from fear of missing you. I could not live without you. I could not think of our bodies parted for even a moment. When in delight the hair of our bodies rose, it seemed like a mountain wall between us. Day and night, we lived that way.

How can I live now?

Rādhā is far away and I in Mathura. And life goes on. A lovely city, the new city-girls and so much wealth around, yet all are useless without Rādhā. My eyes fill with tears. In my startled heart, I hear those girls there and the ripples on the river Jamnā.

Away in Mathura, Krishna recalls Rādhā and the cowgirls and their ardent encounters by the river Jamnā.

NOTES

Poem 22, page 61

> 'As death's agent, the moon shines
> For women parted from their lovers.'

Even in Kālidāsa's time (fourth to fifth century), this dual role of the moon was fully recognized.

> The moon is a pageant of delight for the eyes,
> With rays of light woven into garlands,
> Streaming coolness and ravishing the heart;
> Yet lo! the moon darts fire from frosty beams,
> Burning like a poisoned shaft
> The delicate limbs of the lovely maid
> Pining in separation from her man.
>
> *(The Seasons)*

> 'How can their fragile forms
> Endure such pain?'

So delicate is their beauty, so great their agony.

'Hot grows the sandal paste.' Sandal wood (*chandan*) can be either white or red. The white kind is fragrant. Both are cooling. Sandal paste is made by rubbing a piece of sandal wood on a rough round stone. Flowers are regularly dipped in sandal paste before being offered to an image.

'*Kunda*', *Jasminium pubescens*, a kind of jasmine. Pandit notes that 'it is a short shrub with its stem spirally twisted in rope fashion and with white flowers'.

> Like the gleaming moon,
> The snow, or *kunda* bloom,
> The lovely rope of pearls,
> Where colourful sandal cream is mirrored,
> No more adorns the breasts of elegant maids.

> The gardens are gay with the *kunda* blooms
> White like the gleaming smile of glamorous maids,
> Provoking the mind of love-free saints
> And even more the fancy of love-stained youths.
>
> (KĀLIDĀSA, *The Seasons*)

The moon, sandal paste, pearls and *kunda* flowers were all supposed to be cooling, yet, due to the lady's feverish passion, even these have grown 'hot'.

Poem 25, page 64

'*Jātaki* and *Ketaki*.' 'The *Ketaki*, or screw-pine,' Pandit writes, 'so called because of the curious sedge-like leaves on the summit of its stem, is a large shrub of 15 to 20 feet which extends over a large space by sending down aerial roots from its branches. It blossoms during the rainy season in panicles of large white sheath-like leaves enclosing spongy-looking bundles of closely packed, minute, white flowers. Roxburgh writes: "It is the tender, white leaves of the flowers, chiefly those of the male, that yield the most delightful of fragrance, for which they are so universally and deservedly esteemed. For of all the perfumes in the world, it must be the richest and most powerful." *Kevda* water, like rose water, is a very cooling and popular drink during the summer.' (Pandit, 80)

Poem 52, page 91

'Scratches of nails scarring her firm breasts.' Scratching with the nails was early recognized in India as a potent means for exciting love. The *Kāma Sutra* (third century AD) examines the practice in some detail. Various parts of the body, it declares, need different types of scratch and even nails are of three distinct kinds. Breasts were special targets for a lover's attack—each kind of scratch having its own name. A curved mark impressed on the neck or breasts was called the 'half moon'. A mark in the form of a small line was called a 'line' and this, when curved and made on the breast, was called a 'tiger's nail'. When a curved mark was made on the breasts with five nails, it was called a 'peacock's foot'. This type of scratch was specially prized since it needed great skill to make it properly. Another scratch was called the 'jump of a hare'. This was made with five nails near the nipple. A mark made on the lips or the breasts in the form of a blue lotus was called the 'leaf of a blue lotus'. Scratch marks were often proudly displayed by a girl as proof of her charms.

> 'And then with tender care
> Studies the love-bites on her lower lip.'

Besides scratches, love-bites were also prescribed by the *Kāma Sutra*. Parts that were right for scratching were generally right for kissing, the love-bite being only an intensified form of kiss. Not every part, however, might be bitten. The upper lip, in particular, was spared. Like scratches, love-bites were subjected to the same intense classification. Biting which left only an excessive redness was called the 'hidden bite'. When a bite was made by all the teeth, it was called a 'line of points'. Biting which was done by bringing together the teeth and the lips was called 'the coral and the jewel'. When love-bites formed a circle but showed uneven risings, they were called a 'broken cloud'. Many broad rows of marks near to one another, and with red gaps, were called the 'biting of a boar'. The sort of love-bite appropriate for the lower lip was the 'hidden bite'.

Like Vidyāpati, Kālidāsa also cited love-bites as marks of ardent loving and noticed the mingled pride and confusion with which a girl examined the results of a lover's fury.

> Behold! the young maid, mirror in hand,
> Making up her lotus face
> In the sidelong morning sun;
> Pouting her mouth she scans her lips
> Whose essence was sucked by the lover.
>
> (KĀLIDĀSA, *The Seasons*)

BIBLIOGRAPHY

TEXTS

BANDYOPADHYAY, SAROJ. *Vaishnava Padaratnāvali* (Calcutta, 1961).

BASU, SHANKARI PRASAD. *Chandidās O Vidyāpati* (Calcutta, 1960).

BENIPURI, RAMVRIKSHA. *Vidyāpati ki Padāvali* (Patna, 1925).

JHA, SUBHADRA. *The Songs of Vidyāpati* (Banaras, 1954).

MOZUMDAR, BIMANBIHARI. *Panchshata Batsarer Padāvali* (Calcutta, 1961).
Shodash Shatābdir Padāvali Sāhitya (Calcutta, 1961).

ROY, KALIDAS. *Padāvali Sāhitya* (Calcutta, 1961).

SINHA, KUMAR GANGANAND. *Vidyāpati ki Padāvali* (Laheriasarai, 1925).

GENERAL

ARCHER, W. G. 'Maithil Painting', *Marg* (Bombay, 1948), III, No. 3, 24–33.
The Dove and the Leopard (London, 1948).
Kangra Painting (London, 1952).
Garhwal Painting (London, 1954).
The Loves of Krishna (London, 1957).

ARCHER, W. G. (ed.) *The Kāma Sutra:* trans. Sir Richard Burton and F. F. Arbuthnot (London, 1963).

BASHAM, A. L. *The Wonder that was India* (London, 1954).

CHANDRA, MOTI. 'An Illustrated Set of the Amaru Sataka', *Bulletin of the Prince of Wales Museum of Western India* (Bombay, 1953), No. 2.

ELWIN, VERRIER, AND HIVALE, SHAMRAO. *Folk-Songs of the Maikal Hills* (London, 1944).

ELWIN, VERRIER. *Folk-Songs of Chhattisgarh* (London, 1948).

GRIERSON, G. A. *An Introduction to the Maithili Language* (Calcutta, 1882).
The Modern Vernacular Literature of Hindustan (Calcutta, 1889).

KEITH, A. B. *History of Sanskrit Literature* (Oxford, 1928).

KEYT, G. *Shri Jayadeva's Gita Govinda* (Bombay, 1947).

MACDONELL, A. A. *History of Sanskrit Literature* (London, 1900).

MATHERS, E. POWYS (trans.) *Eastern Love* (London, 1927–30). *Love Songs of Asia* (London, 1944).

MEYER, J. J. *Sexual Life in Ancient India* (second ed. London, 1952).

PANDIT, R. S. (trans.) *Ritusamhāra or the Pageant of the Seasons* (Bombay, 1947).

PEIRIS, H., AND VAN GEYZEL, L. C. (trans.) *Kālidāsa: The Seasons, the Ornament of Love, the Broken Pot* (Colombo, 1961).

RANDHAWA, M. S. *The Krishna Legend in Pahāri Painting* (New Delhi, 1956).
Kangra Paintings of the Bhāgavata Purāna (New Delhi, 1960).
Kangra Paintings on Love (New Delhi, 1962).
Kangra Paintings of the Gita Govinda (New Delhi, 1963).

SEN, D. C. *History of Bengali Language and Literature* (Calcutta, 1911).

INDEX